MOSAICS

Ferdinando Rossi

MOSAICS

A Survey
of their
History and
Techniques

PRAEGER PUBLISHERS
New York · Washington · London

Translated from the Italian by David Ross

Published in the United States of America in 1970
by Praeger Publishers, Inc.
111 Fourth Avenue, New York, N.Y. 10003

All rights reserved

©1968 by Alfieri & Lacroix Editore, Milan

©English translation 1970 by Pall Mall Press, London

Library of Congress Catalog Card Number: 72-89606

Printed in Italy

CONTENTS

	Preface	6
I	**Mosaics**	7

    What Mosaics are 7
    Origins and Early Diffusion in the East 13
    The Mosaics of Rome 17   Roman Domination 35
    Mosaics in Christian Art 37
    Aquileia 38   Ravenna 43   Venice 47
    Tuscany 53   Rome 63   Sicily 74
    Diffusion and Decadence of Christian Mosaic Work 76
    Cosmati Work 88

II	**Intarsio Work**	90
III	**Hard Stones**	105
IV	**Commesso Work**	117
	Glossary	182
	Notes	187
	Bibliography	194
	Sources of Illustrations	195
	Index of Names and Places	196

PREFACE

The following study of Mosaics is intended to illustrate the development of the art from its origins up to the present time.

The study begins with a historical analysis of the various kinds of mosaic work, and hence of *intarsio* work – a decorative craft closely allied to mosaic yet quite distinct from it. The process of development of mosaic and intarsio is pursued to the stage where *commesso* work evolved; which later achieved its finest expression in work in hard stone. Such work in hard stone is clearly differentiated from previous achievements both by the technical difficulties involved in its manufacture and by the distinct artistic style it assumes. The choice of each piece is dictated by considerations beyond those of following a preconceived pattern, and so requires a finer hand than that demanded for the composition of tesserae over a paper pattern – a procedure always possible with marble, vitreous paste, glazed tesserae or soft stones, where there is absolute uniformity of colour and hence no need for specialised and imaginative skill.

The opportunity has been taken to provide the student with information not only as to the names of the so-called hard stones (*pietre dure*), but also as to their chemico-physical structures and their places in mineralogy and geology: for without such information it is quite impossible to form a clear idea of the complexities of the craft.

Also discussed are the various techniques used by the craftsman, together with some of the tools that have been widely employed in ancient and modern times.

The text is illustrated by a collection of colour and monochrome plates of mosaics and famous *commesso* work, which show the very fine effects that the craftsmen of the past were able to obtain, especially when they worked with hard stone; such effects still have the power to astound us across the centuries with their freshness and vivacity.

Florence, December 1968

I. MOSAICS

What Mosaics Are

The word mosaic derives etymologically from *musa* (*opus musivum*). In Italian in fact the word *musaico* occurs sometimes, although *mosaico* is much more common and seems to have originated in Roman times. If we seek to understand the original motives for choosing this particular means of expression which has attracted so many artists since such remote times, we should first remember that man, in ornamenting his buildings and giving visual expression to his imagination, has always sought to employ materials that will withstand the test of time for as long as possible. Colours applied with a brush are not entirely satisfactory in this respect. Even though various artifices may be used to lend them more stability, they suffer from a certain frailty. The ingenious process, for example, by which the colours are applied directly to the fresh plaster so that they partake of the phenomenon of crystallisation – true fresco painting – has a life span limited to that of the film of plaster covering the wall, which is itself fatally exposed to the inclemencies of the weather on an exterior surface, and, even on an interior surface, subject to the vicissitudes of fortune.

Mosaic on the other hand has always given the impression of greater stability; perhaps wrongly, because it partly depends upon the plasters and cements that support it and so is subject to the effect of time. In mosaic pictorial work too there is dependence upon pigments (usually derived from earths or inorganic materials mixed with water, oil or various other glues and fixatives) laid upon small regular or irregular pieces of resistant material (stone, marble, terracotta, glass, enamelled paste, etc.) which have been disposed side by side with one another, generally in some prearranged and regular shape.

The pieces themselves were known to the Greeks as *abakischoi*, and to the Romans as *abaculi*, *tesserae*, or more commonly *tessellae*; for which reason the *opera musiva* in which they were employed became known as *opus tesselatum*. If, however, the individual pieces had a varied form, the mosaic was called *opus vermiculatum*, *opus sectile*, etc., according to the special features it introduced.

The pieces are usually fixed to the structural base by means of gum mastic or simply with cement, and the artists placed – and in some cases still do – the tesserae one by one in the fresh plaster, following a pattern which they themselves may have traced in the plaster. They can alter the effect of the pattern according to their taste, by varying the plane of the surface in relation to the plane of the base, so that the incidence of the light is

7

1 Opus alexandrinum. *The design is obtained by means of irregular tesserae disposed in such a way that the base shows through.*

altered and in consequence its reflection as viewed by the observer. Naturally such techniques are especially effective where the tesserae are not opaque or dull, but are rather of such materials as vitreous pastes, enamels or hard stones, with smooth and shiny surfaces.

Backgrounds may be uniformly gilded, or else gold is used in particular areas to give prominence to detail; such devices are often used, and tesserae are made specially for the purpose, a slender sheet of gold being sandwiched in glass and fired in appropriate kilns until the whole is practically fused, giving a rigid, homogeneous tesserae.

The basal cement employed may vary considerably. The ancient Romans used *pozzolana*, marble or brick dust, slaked lime and water, mixed in proportions which varied according to the kind of work in hand and local conditions. This mixture would be laid out in a bed and allowed to harden. Then various systems were used for the tracing of the design which was to serve as a guide. In the past the most popular method was to cover the base with a stratum of gesso of the same thickness as the tesserae themselves. The design would be traced on this surface and the tesserae placed in position without actually being fixed to it. The gesso was then gradually removed down to the basal cement, the resulting cavity being carefully filled with a fresh stratum of very fine and liquid cement. It was in this that the tesserae were finally applied and allowed to adhere, after which the final processes of work on the mosaic itself could begin. This explains why many ancient pavements may show a residuum of gesso: it was used, not as is often thought, as a cement, but purely in an intermediary process. During the late period of decadence of the antique mosaic art, the enormous demand

2   Opus tesselatum. *The tesserae are almost identical and cut regularly.*

3   Opus sectile. *Small tesserae have been replaced here by large areas of coloured marble.*

for pavements was met by the formation of an organisation of mosaic craftsmen, who avoided the lengthy procedure required to place each single tessera in position, and instead simply applied the tesserae back to front on a sheet of paper on which the design had been traced, and to which had been applied a glue easily soluble in water. The whole thing was then placed upon the fresh plaster, with the paper surface on the outside. As soon as the plaster had dried so that the tesserae were fixed in position, the paper was removed by wetting it, and, section by section, the panel was placed in position. This method, not infrequently employed today, gives a flat, smooth surface to the work which quite lacks the sense of movement obtained by the method first described.

The form of the elements used distinguishes the various kinds of mosaic, each of which has its own name deriving from Roman times. *Opus alexandrinum* (Plate 1) is a pavement mosaic made from small elements, some black and some white, usually quadrangular in shape and rather thin, scattered in a pattern on a background which is almost invariably red in colour. In *opus tesselatum* (Plate 2) the design is composed of quadrangular tesserae cut at right angles to the plane of view. *Opus vermiculatum* on the other hand contains not only cubic tesserae, but various other shapes, which are placed in rows, twisting and coiling like worms (*vermi*) so as better to define the outline of the designs. This is now clearly a very different craft from what it was when interpreted according to the most ancient Roman tradition. With the latter not only marbles and enamelled elements were used, but also gemstones, such as lapis lazuli, jasper, cornelian, alabaster, agate and onyx, besides vitreous pastes and – more rarely – terracotta pieces. These would be cut according to the needs of the craftsman, varying both in size and shape according to requirement, and were sometimes reduced to the most minute fragments to obtain tonality and other effects. By such means it was possible to approximate the fine figural effects of painting.

Opus signinum, almost always used for paving, may be of Greek origin,[1] the original version being the *pavimentum barbaricum*. It is made up of river pebbles roughly arranged into patterns and cemented in lime or clay.

In antiquity in Italy a mixture of *cocciopesto* (crushed potsherds) and lime was first made up which gave a very resistant pinky colour (*pavimentum testaceum*). Into this bed were introduced either pebbles or coarse chips of porphyry and marble (*opus segmentatum*). Segmental mosaics of this kind attributed to the first century of the Empire are to be seen between the basilica and the campanile at Aquileia, at the earliest level of excavation there.[2]

Opus sectile (Plate 3), finally, differs substantially from all other systems in that it represents a different approach to the problem of producing figural work that resembles painting as nearly as possible. In it, coloured marbles and sometimes also hard stones were employed, each piece being cut according to the outline of the desired design. Since it lacked chiaroscuro, the work had uniform colouration, rather like a rough sketch for a painting.

Almost all the earliest mosaics that have come down to us are pavement mosaics, and were from the first called *lithostrotum* from the Greek *lithostrotos* (from *lithos*, stone, and *stroo*, pavement). The term made no reference to the type of materials employed, since 'stone' was used indiscriminately for any lapidary material.

4 *Half columns covered with mosaic made of conical terracotta tesserae. Uruk (Mesopotamia), beginning of the second millennium B.C.*

Gullini[3] reports on this matter that even Pliny makes a clear distinction between *pavimenta* and *lithostrata*, a distinction which has its roots in etymology. The former suggests by its root *pav*, common both to Greek and Latin, a beaten pavement, as is explained in further paragraphs of Pliny's text.[4] One is dealing thus with a pavement of beaten lime or stucco, made with a technique similar to that used for wall plaster. ... All the various types of *opus signinum*, made by beating the base of *cocciopesto*, belong to pavements. *Lithostrata* on the other hand, as the term suggests, are types of paving undertaken with the tessellation of small fragments of stone. Thus the distinction is made between paving constructed with the same technique as plaster, and that made with small elements closely placed next to one another. The same author then quotes Pliny's words: 'The *lithostrata* started to be made as far back as the time of Sulla; the one which he had made for the Sanctuary of Fortuna at Praeneste, with little marble tesserae, is still in existence.'

Where a decoration in a mosaic pavement is described as *emblemata*, this refers to the form of the design, and suggests an emblem in the centre, or else some well-outlined design, possibly enclosed by a frame; around this and over the rest of the surface there would be various forms of decoration, mostly geometric.

Two famous *emblemata* mosaics of the third century B.C. are those of the 'comic musicians' at Pompeii and of the Roman *asarotos oikos* (uncleaned) now in the Lateran Museum. The former is attributed to Dioscorides of Samos; the latter perhaps to a native of Alexandria or, more probably, to Sosos of Pergamon, whom Pliny mentions as the inventor of this *triclinium* (dining-hall) type of pavement.[5] The colour and design of this was meant to give the impression of an uncleaned floor so as to allow guests to throw down rubbish from the table without any inhibitions.[6] Sosos of Pergamon refined and idealised this intensely prosaic device.

No materials may be regarded as specially suitable for mosaics since the most varied substances have always been used – marbles, hard stones, seashells, vitreous pastes, terracotta, mother of pearl – according to what was available in the neighbourhood, and to what effects the craftsman wished to obtain.

As has already been mentioned, the great aspiration of mosaic craftsmen had always been to equal the fine effects of painting. This has been attempted in two different ways: the first was to break up the individual tesserae into minute fragments a few millimetres in breadth; the second was to enlarge them so as to provide large, well defined areas of colour. Neither method, however, could produce the fine results that were later to be obtained by exploiting the natural colours and configurations which occur in hard stones.

Origins and Early Diffusion in the East

The experts are all in agreement that mosaic work must have had its origin in the East, but there is far less certainty about the date at which it was first practised. It is easy to imagine the excitement of those who first stumbled upon the system of producing the almost incorruptible, shining surface of a mosaic. The ease with which varying the plane of exposure of the various elements would produce brilliant and mysterious effects made this art a natural complement to that of architecture. While it is known that the Chaldeans were skilled mosaicists already by 2500 B.C., the art was not much employed by the Persians, Assyrians or Babylonians. Fasolo[7] says that 'it is common in Chaldean architecture to find mud walls decorated by a curious mosaic of lively colours. The work was produced by inserting in the wall itself many clay cones, the bases of which had been painted black, red or yellow, which glowed on the surface with strange and fascinating effect' (Plate 4).

Among the most ancient mosaic decorations is that which comes from a pre-dynastic tomb at Ur and which represents a feast after a victory.

'At Uruk, the modern Warka, to the north of Ur, homeland of the hero Gilgamesh who has inspired so many works of art, are to be seen the limestone block foundations of a most ancient palace, together with another, known as that of Eanna, with a ziggurat.'[8]

As a result of research undertaken at the end of the last century objects of great archeological value were discovered in tombs, amongst which was the so-called 'Standard of Ur'. This consists of two rectangular panels, the first showing scenes of war and the second scenes of peace (Plate 5), each in three horizontal registers.

From the very first it was believed that these were portable panels, the more so because they were found next to the right shoulder of a corpse, as though they had been buried along with their bearer. They are perhaps the most ancient example of portable mosaics we know, and their structure deserves particular attention. As mentioned above, each panel is divided into three registers; each of these is bordered by fragments of sea-shell, whilst decoration within them is composed of pieces of stone, mother-of-pearl and clay. These may not be considered as tesserae in the proper sense, but constitute an example of *opus sectile*,[9] since the various

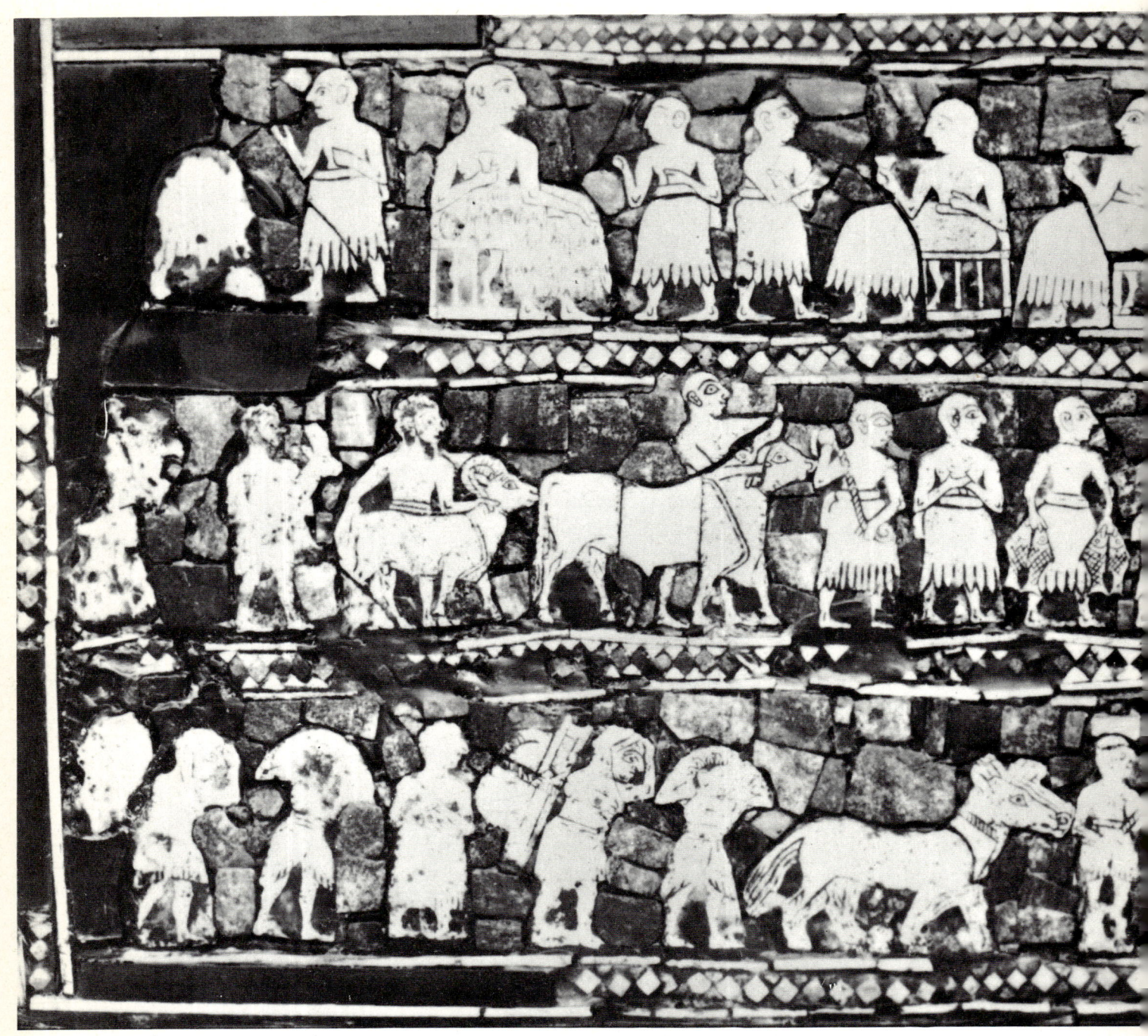

5 *The 'Standard of Ur' (third millennium B.C.), made of semi-precious materials cut in the same manner as the Roman opus sectile. London, British Museum.*

elements have been cut and shaped from materials planed in advance and reduced to a very small thickness. Originally all the pieces were fixed to wooden boards by means of an impasto of bitumen, of which some dried-up remains were found. The whole composition, however, was much damaged either by the complete destruction of its

wooden support or as a result of the collapse of the roof of the tomb or both. During the extremely difficult reconstruction work various mistakes were made, and certain irregularities are still to be seen; nonetheless the historical value of the pieces is self-evident, for they date the art of mosaics back into the third millenium B.C. at least.

It is considered unlikely that the 'Standard' was the only example of its kind to have been made, even if it is the only one to have survived into modern times. Its particular importance is that this is not simply a piece of decorative material, but a descriptive work which reveals the efficacy of the art both as to its powers of longevity and as an expressive document of a period so remote as to leave us few pictorial records. To find a work which adopts this system and with such considerable artistic success again, we shall have to wait for several thousand years – in fact for the Roman period itself. But the 'Standard of Ur' is not interesting only for its artistic merits, but also for the techniques that were employed and the materials used in its construction. Even the means by which the borders are shaped at the corners by the positioning of the tiny squared tesserae follows a technique used in relatively recent work so closely as to appear to have been copied.

This, the most ancient visual record we possess of the soldiers and citizens of Sumeria, shows how human taste repeats itself over enormous distances of time – and this is so natural a thing that it may almost be taken for granted.

The Egyptians decorated their palaces and temples with mosaics; vitreous enamel and incrustations of the same material were in use from the earliest dynasties. Here too, Pliny is of assistance to us for he attributes the invention of glass to the merchants of 'natron'.[10] During the Hellenistic period, at the time of the Ptolemies, the glass industry flourished, and it is said that Hieron II, a tyrant of Syracuse, sent Ptolemy III of Alexandria ships decorated with mosaics representing scenes from the Iliad, the work of two artists living in Sicily – Archimedes and Archia of Corinth. Ptolemy IV Philopater believed that these were of finer *commesso* work than had hitherto been produced in Egypt; so he had a ship built with columns and cabins of mosaic.[11] From all this it seems probable that enamel and vitreous paste mosaics arrived in Italy from Egypt after the refined Alexandrian civilisation had carried the art to a high degree of perfection. Examples of the enamelled tesserae known as *vitrum* were apparently to be found right up to the twelfth century.

Few mosaic monuments have come to light in Egypt, but these few are all of fine quality. There is for example a mosaic with an allegorical head of Alexandria signed by Sophilos, and another of similar provenance showing scenes on the Nile (found at Tell Timai in the Delta, now in the Alexandria Museum).[12]

In this same city the art of mosaics developed alongside the other forms of art and from there was carried in two directions: first, eastwards towards Syria (where its destiny was mediocre), Asia Minor and Byzantium (where, on the other hand, an exceptionally fine mosaic art developed), and second towards Magna Graecia and thence to Italy.

Mario Bussagli[13] writes that 'on both internal and external walls of buildings in Iran, mosaic has been much used since extremely ancient times; we may regard the similar plastic decoration of Elamite temples, though it is monochromatic, as evidence of tendencies in this direction; we know from various sources that during the Parthian period, and above all during the Sassanian period (which dynasty began in 226 B.C.) internal decoration often consisted of a tessellation of glass or coloured paste. It was logical that in such circumstances the technique of mosaic should develop particularly well.' It is important to note that even at this remote period of antiquity glass mosaic was used and the technique of manufacturing the tesserae of this material was already understood. Glass tesserae figure also in two important monuments of truly exceptional interest: in the Dome of the Rock in Jerusalem and in the great mosque at Damascus,[14] which is of the Ommayad epoch anterior to 750. These are mosaics of polychrome tesserae, the dominating motifs being

6 *Overleaf: Battle between Macedonians and Persians. Mosaic from the House of the Faun, Pompeii.*

flowers in fields of gold on deep blue backgrounds, and decorated with green acanthus leaves.

There are tesserae of marble or other lapidary material (although probably not of hard stone) in medieval eastern mosaics, and such materials were very widely used in paving mosaics in place of glass, perhaps for practical reasons. Such materials were only later used in mural mosaics. It is to the Mameluk artists, chosen from the Turkish armies which were in general recruited from slaves (*mamluk*) and who gave their name to the dominant class in Egypt from 1250 to 1517, that we owe the mosaic decorations in marble tesserae of various sizes, and usually in the form of triangles, stars and rectangles, yellow, red, black and white in colour.

As for enamelled ceramic from which tesserae came to be made for mural decoration, it appears that its practice was initiated in the twelfth century by the Seljuk Turks – the sultans who overwhelmed the Gasnavid dynasty, rulers of the Bagdhad Caliphate.[15]

In the blue mosque of Tabriz, provincial capital of Azerbaijan in Persia, there are panels in the shape of scrolls or stars which date back to 1437–1477. Dimand asserts that 'the art of ceramic mosaics reached its apogee' in the fourteenth century in Persia under the Turkish Caliphate of the Safavids. At the end of the sixteenth century and in the first half of the seventeenth during the period of Shah Abbas the Great (who had some connection with Italy through Pietro della Valle), and perhaps as a result of the considerable commercial development he encouraged in his country, great mural mosaics show such far flung eastern influence as that of China. Herman Goetz[16] suggests that mosaics were introduced into India during the Islamic period – that is after the tenth century. He also suggests that diffusion of the art took place in areas enjoying the driest climate, since 'the wide variations in temperature and humidity which are characteristic of the Indian climate are inimical to the preservation of such work, especially in the case of painted tiles'. The latter were in use in India during the fifteenth century, and figure for the first time at the principal gate of the Fort of Jaipur, and thereafter, as true mosaic work where the pieces themselves have been cut, in the tomb of Sikandar Jodi who died in 1517.

Tiles as mosaic elements appear in India in the sixteenth century, and soon after stone tesserae begin to be employed – these probably being imported from Persia. They are generally restricted to the Punjab region, with rare appearances in Delhi and Agra.

In the Fort at Lahore, built during the first half of the seventeenth century, mosaics of various stone tesserae were used to depict scenes of war with elephants and soldiers.

Geotz mentions that mosaics of small tesserae and cubes of stone are to be found in the Mosque of Ser Sah at Purana Kila (Delhi), and he notes in these Mameluk and Egyptian influence.

From 1556 to 1605, during the reign of Akbar, and from 1605 to 1627 during that of Jahangir, such mosaic decoration was widely diffused; in later periods it was replaced by *intarsio*.

Among the most important Hellenistic centres, was Pergamon, capital of Mysia, which had an important school around the master Sosos.

The Mosaics of Rome

Mosaic work seems to have first appeared in Rome during the time of the third Punic War (half way through the second century B.C.).

Its greatest period of development, however, occurred during Imperial times.

'The Romans were great masters of painting. This truth, evident to anyone who considers the frescoes in the buildings at Pompeii and Herculaneum, or in the Roman villas and imperial palaces, is not one that all students are ready to accept or even to criticise.'[17]

Naturally enough there were in ancient Rome both masters and minor artists, as occurs throughout the history of art. Both Hellenistic and oriental tendencies are to be found in mosaics as also in mural painting; given the relationship that Rome maintained with the Greek world and the Orient in general it is natural enough that these should appear. A vast number of Roman mosaics have been preserved for us, and they display all kinds of decoration, figurative and abstract in both pavement and mural work. The most common technique employed is that of composition with mosaic tesserae, in all the varieties that have been discussed earlier. Colours are obtained with various marbles or vitreous pastes. Comparatively few mosaics display large gilded areas, for which reason those which do contain tesserae with gold leaf are particularly significant. By no means were all the artists famous. Very often, indeed, the work would be undertaken by a simple craftsman, especially in the case of ordinary ornamental pavements of no particular importance, which were decorated with traditional designs; the workman, once he had learned how to compose these, could repeat them endlessly. Mosaic work was not only used in pavements, since we have numerous examples of mural panels. Pavement work, however, does predominate over mural work, the latter being most commonly found on vaults and arches. The reader's attention will

7 *Marine fauna on a Roman mosaic. Naples, National Museum.*

be directed to the most accessible works, generally to be found in the large centres of habitation, since the scope of the present work does not permit exhaustive analysis of individual and minor pieces.

Many figurative mosaics were discovered during the excavations at Pompeii, almost all the finest being from the famous House of the Faun, which was built during the first century B.C.

These works deserve particular attention as they will help our understanding of successive developments considerably. The most famous example of all is the panel depicting

the battle between the Macedonians and the Persians (Plate 6). It was made during the second century B.C., but probably copies a painting of the fourth century B.C. According to Ducati[18] it is not known which battle is depicted, although it is generally assumed to be the Battle of Issos, November 333 B.C. Rizzo[19] is convinced that it is indeed this particular battle that is shown, and finds similarities with the decorations of Diodorus Siculus and Quintus Curtius.

As to who was the author of the original painting of which the mosaic is a copy, Rizzo writes of three painters who at the beginning

8 *Cats, birds and fish on a Roman mosaic. Naples, National Museum.*

of the hellenistic period painted the Battle of Alexander with the Persians. He disregards the attribution to Aristeides of Thebes on the grounds that the source is unreliable, preferring Pliny who cites Philoxenus of Eritrea as the painter of pictures of similar battles. As a third hypothesis Rizzo considers the evidence of Ptolemy of Hephaestion concerning the artist Helena, daughter of the Egyptian Timon, and a contemporary of the event. This theory too has its objections arising principally from doubts as to whether 'such a large and powerful rendering of a scene of battle could be the work of a woman'. He further explains that there are four colours used in the mosaic: white, yellow, red and black. It is at least certain that the work has given rise to great discussion and research from the most ancient times onwards.

Gullini[20] mentions the mosaic as one of the most precious Hellenistic pieces, and asserts that the work may probably be attributed to Philoxenus of Eritrea.

Gerspach,[21] however, comes to an entirely different conclusion. He believes that the subject is the Battle of Arbela, in which Alexander defeated Darius in the autumn of 331 B.C. He offers in evidence the figure of a warrior, who may be Darius, and who is fleeing in his war chariot. Gerspach finds this figure particularly impressive among the others in the mêlée of the battle, and he concludes that only a great artist could have rendered it so effectively. He writes: 'The mosaicist charged with the work understood how difficult this particular subject was. His tesserae are of a maximum width of three millimetres; marbles are mixed among vitreous pastes and all tightly packed, so that he has produced the effect of a painting with surprising skill. It is possible to argue that the original painting was larger than the mosaic, since the mosaic figures are about two-thirds natural size. It is also quite probable that the picture that served as model was itself only a copy. The composition, design and general character of the "Battle of Arbela" is so superior to any other work in Pompeii that it should without any doubt be assigned to a very important Greek artist, possibly Helena, sister(?) of Timon and a contemporary of Alexander. The work was found in the House of the Faun in 1830.'

This detailed criticism has been included here because, apart from the attribution (for which we cannot assume any responsibility), it offers material which is useful to the present study. Gerspach observes that the tesserae are tiny, and confirms the contention maintained elsewhere in this study that the earliest mosaicists also attempted to achieve pictorial effects by breaking up the tesserae almost to dust. In doing so they came close to the effect they sought; but such efforts involved misuse of the materials, and so entirely missed those special visual results which may be achieved with mosaics alone, and which may never be obtained with a brush. The colouring and design, on the other hand, respect the rules of perspective which were subsequently lost and which were rediscovered only much later with the advent of the Renaissance.

The other picture discussed here also comes from the House of the Faun, although it is now in the National Museum of Naples, and is according to Ducati[22] of Alexandrian origin. Like the preceding piece, it is the work of an artist who was very thoroughly acquainted with the art of still life; and he too has employed mosaic as a medium of expression akin to painting. He has left us a work of great artistic value which heralds a style of the distant future, that of the seventeenth and eighteenth centuries. It is certain of course

9 *Nilotic scene. Mosaic from the Sanctuary of Fortuna Primigenia, Praeneste.*

that the art of painting was well known in antiquity, since many examples of great artistic value have been brought to light. But mosaicists, working with vitreous materials, were conscious of the fact that these materials also lent themselves beautifully to faithfully reproducing for instance the scales of fish, the feathers of birds or the fur of a cat. Thus it is that the history of mosaics begins in Italy with these fine pictorial effects, and ends there with other fine effects obtained through use of the natural variegations of stones.

Representation of animals is widely diffused in ancient painting and is connected with the rendering of landscape and still life.[23] In Hellenistic painting in particular it constitutes a mode all on its own, and the same Sosos of Pergamon is famous as the painter of the doves which are to be found again in mosaic work – this time, however, used as a Christian symbol, yet in the same pose, drinking at the edge of a bowl. As a result of the conquests of Alexander of Macedonia the Greeks were able to observe wild beasts which had hitherto been unknown, and these fired the imagination of Greek artists who depicted them fighting among themselves or in combat with men. This explains why so many are found at Pompeii and in Hadrian's villa, the most famous of these is illustrated in this book (Plate 6). Rizzo compares such scenes, frequently depicted in the so-called *Xenia* of the ancient Greeks, with the picture by Pireicus who may have been a contemporary of Alexander the Great. He is mentioned by Pliny as the author of small grotesque or unpretentious works such as still-lives, and was therefore known as *riparografo*, or the 'wretched composer'. At Pompeii during the period of the early style, *Xenia* are to be found only in mosaic work; and the one showing a cat attacking a quail below which are wild duck, fish, other birds and shells (Plate 8), is among the most ancient: – 'an Alexandrian copy of Alexandrian art'. Mosaics depicting not only beasts but also fish are diffused right across the ancient world; a famous one is illustrated here, which also comes from the House of the Faun at Pompeii, showing a battle between a lobster and an octopus (Plate 7) – a ubiquitous theme in the ancient world. In this piece the subjects are beautifully composed and much effect has been obtained by the skilful placing of coloured tesserae of various size. Also reproduced are mosaics of various species of fish, executed with such spectacular verisimilitude that even at a distance of so many centuries, an ichthyologist can recognise each with ease. The same skill is evident in the manner in which the tone and irridescence of the water and the coloured scales of the fish are realised. These beautiful compositions were in great demand in the Roman world, as decorations for the villas and houses of patricians.

Critics have complained of a certain affectation in the carefully presented forms and details, which however seem almost impossible to realise with tesserae. But the interplay of the particles of marble and vitreous paste reveal themselves as incomparably suitable materials for rendering depth in landscapes – and they are even more successful in seascapes where they can give the illusion of glittering light. With these, as with other less successful 'pictures in stone' there is above all a vivacity which occurs but rarely in oil or fresco painting.

This vivacity was exploited countless times in the use of such mosaics to decorate the ornamental pools of Roman villas where the shimmering effect would be increased by the water itself in the sunlight. Similarly the

25

10 *Nilotic scene on a pavement mosaic. Sanctuary of Fortuna Primigenia, Praeneste.*

custom of paving the *impluvium* of ancient houses with mosaic reveals the same taste for a medium which was altered and made more interesting in appearance when it was rained upon.

According to Gullini there certainly operated in Rome at this period a team of mosaicists who knew well what had been accomplished in Greece both aesthetically and technically. Perhaps it was to this same team that we owe the mosaics of the Sanctuary of Fortuna Primigenia at Praeneste.[24]

'In those parts which are without doubt of ancient workmanship and which are made entirely with marble, without any intrusion of vitreous pastes, the two mosaics at Praeneste seem to constitute examples of that type of *lithostroton* in which the pavement is entirely covered with small tesserae.' (Plates 9, 10.) Gullini[25] gives a detailed and accurate description of the mosaics of Praeneste – both of the so-called fish and nilotic pieces, and his description of the technique and theme favoured by these great Roman artists will repay careful study.

The major objective of this eminent scholar was to establish the authentic parts of the work following the numerous restorations undertaken by Cardinal Francesco Barberini during 1640, the year in which the mosaics (having in 1625 been removed and presented to Barberini by Cardinal Andrea Peretti) were re-installed at Praeneste. After restoration the mosaics were replaced at ground-floor level in the monument on the basis of a design by Cassiano del Pozzo. A final restoration was undertaken in Rome in the mosaic studios of St Peter's under the aegis of Giovanni Azurrio. They were then once more returned to Praeneste in 1855, and they remained there until 1943. In that year they were removed again to Rome for the duration of the war, after which they were finally installed in a suitable room of the Palazzo Baronale at Praeneste. Gullini comes to the conclusion that the major restoration was that undertaken by Calandra in 1640. But in view of the restless life the work has been

forced to lead, it is clear that this judgement was not an easy one to reach.

Illustrated in the present volume is one of the pieces that has remained complete. The scene depicts a cottage and a castle where black and white birds are shown on the group of buildings (Plate 10).

The mosaics of Praeneste are of the highest quality, and their importance as documentary evidence of Hellenistic mosaic art is exceptional. Gullini observes a close similarity between these works and the mosaic of Alexander, whether in the identical quality of the stones used or in the technique of

11 *Mosaic from Ostia in which tiny tesserae were used to produce minute details.*

shattering certain tesserae. Gullini's conclusion that both sets of work were produced by the same Alexandrian mosaicists is important not only to the critics of the Praeneste pieces, but is also of great interest to the general student of the development of mosaic art in Rome and Italy.

The various evidence that Gullini calls upon – and especially the evidence of colouration – lends great weight to his belief in the Alexandrian origin of this school of mosaicists, who, following the route already suggested, moved from Egypt to Rome, where they began their work with the masterpieces we have examined. It is normal enough that the rapid spread in popularity of this type of decoration should have led to its impoverishment to the point of becoming the work of simple copyists.

The similar designs and the presence of Egyptian landscape in these pieces is obviously not entirely coincidental, even if 'it is true that nilotic subjects were common in the repertory of late Hellenistic artists, especially where these had some connection with the Alexandrian aspect of the art'.[26]

Such remarks are all the more interesting when one considers the date cited above from reference to Pliny for the beginning of the mosaic art in Rome.

From the description of the authentic and restored parts of the Praeneste works, and from the freshness of design of the former and clumsiness of the latter, it is easy to deduce that the original was the work of a master-artist who did not leave the reproduction of his designs to the undiscerning hands of his assistants. The impression of freshness remains – one which was to disappear from later works as conditions of life changed and mannerists and inferior copyists dominated the scene.

Gullini considers the theories of *pictura compendiaria*, and believes that research into effects of light must have influenced the makers of the mosaics of Praeneste; whence he feels that the term 'impressionist' may be justifiably applied to it. In this connection he writes: 'It is above all the mosaic of the Nile which seems to me to exemplify perfectly the much discussed "antique expression".' We have seen how, in it, all preoccupation with design has been overcome, whether as to composition or as to perspective, by abandoning all traditional norms. The result is an apparently simplified descriptive summary which owes its success to those effects of light through which the pictorial representation is truly composed.'[27] Perhaps only with mosaic could a work of such power be achieved – and then only at the hands of a master. From such an early date as the first century B.C. few works have survived to testify to this flowering of the art of mosaics. Later, almost mysteriously, mosaic art was to decline both in design and workmanship, even in Rome, where it became victim of its own enormous success, and where there was not a house that could not boast a room paved with mosaic. Except for a few pieces, for which the resources of a master were called upon, such pavements and murals show not merely lack of imagination as to subject matter, but are in their execution clearly the work of simple craftsmen who copied the work of others and who, lacking the skill and inclination to undertake the painstaking labour of making up fine mosaics, produced uneven, coarse work.

Until the first century B.C. mosaics were not much employed, and were considered a luxury which by no means everyone could afford. It was only with time that they became more generally used as floors and re-

placed the less durable and less pleasing concrete. At first geometric patterns and stylised motifs were chosen, then large neutral central spaces, while the borders were decorated with repetitive motifs which were on the whole monochromatic. Sometimes two colours – black and white – were used; and, very occasionally, polychromatic designs were employed.

With the passage of time the number of mosaics increased throughout Italy, and from about 40 B.C. Rome became the principal

centre of production. Decorations became increasingly rich and, while 'emblematic' work tended to diminish, by the time of Augustus the decoration was extended to cover the whole of the paving area. At this time too animal and human motifs are introduced, although always in black on a white background; and this mode continues right up to Claudian times. Typical examples are the mosaics of Ostia (Plate 11).

Giovanni Becatti[28] writes:

'Ostia was, as it were, the wholesale quarter

12 *Large Roman pavement mosaic. Constanta (Black Sea).*

of Rome. It differed from the capital only in its particular commercial function; and for the rest it partook of the tenor of life and culture of the capital. Its inhabitants were neither patricians, nor personalities of the Imperial Court nor plebeians, but rather a lively bourgeoisie whose activities were directed towards the port which formed the commercial capital of the entire Mediterranean basin.'

These inhabitants numbered perhaps forty thousand in the second century, and showed modest pretensions toward the decoration of homes that were never luxurious. Becatti continues:

'This was a comfortable middle class which at no time during the Imperial period preoccupied itself with the refinements of mosaic art or required special designs or emblems of its mosaicists; rather was it content with whatever the local contractor had decided to order from the local workmen.' And again: 'The only exception to this rule is to be found in the rich and monumental complex of the Palace excavated by Visconti at the centre of the previously unexplored zone between the present western boundary of the *via della Foce* and *Tor Bovacciano*. This edifice, at first called the '*Palazzo di Gamala*' and later *Palazzo Imperiale*, has baths and a Mithraeum attached. These are decorated with polychromatic and black and white mosaics, which were constructed during the Antonine period. The luxury and fine workmanship of these mosaics contrasts noticeably with the modest pieces to be found elsewhere in the town.'

It is interesting to note that the mosaics at Ostia generally show uniformity of workmanship and technique. Thus, the foundation of the mosaic itself is laid upon a base of broken tuff 'about 20 to 25 centimetres in depth, which is covered by a shallow covering of *pozzolana* (volcanic dust), one half to one centimetre thick, which lends a certain elasticity to the overlying stratum of mortar of lime and marble dust. Into this the tesserae are inserted, all being of precisely the same length'. As for the material of which the tesserae are made, Becatti goes on to say that the white 'are in general of calcareous stone which lends itself to a simple, clean cut. Only in mosaics of the late third and fourth centuries A.D. does one find the use of marble tesserae, which were always used in limited fashion and in large pieces. Other tesserae are not always of dark grey or black flint. Coloured tesserae are generally made from local stone; the most popular colours are: brick red or pink, pale yellow, ochre, greenish, and pale blue-grey. To these are added, especially in mosaics of the third and fourth centuries, various marble tesserae, particularly *Portasanta*, antique yellow, cipolin and antique rose. Serpentine is very rarely used, as it is too hard to be cut regularly. The use of vitreous pastes in paving mosaics is rather limited; they are to be found in some of the finer work of the second century A.D., and are generally more common in wall mosaic.'

These observations show that there existed in the Roman period – especially in Rome itself, which was so rich in mural mosaics – a current system of mosaic techniques which was also to be found in areas distant from Rome. Becatti himself dissents somewhat from Gullini's interpretation of Pliny's text; yet it seems hard to deny that even pavement mosaics of quite modest simplicity of decoration may be considered pictorial expressions in a broad sense. It is interesting that an artistic taste must have prevailed which demanded that a tone should be infused into the walls that differed from the

13 *Detail of a large Roman pavement mosaic. Constanta (Black Sea).*

paving – a contrast that might be continued in the furnishing. All this is not to belittle the attentive researches of Becatti into Pliny's text – researches that reach far beyond the scope of this study, limited as it is to mosaic work. We entirely agree, however, on his interpretation of the term *vermiculatum*; it does indeed seem to refer to the technical structure of the tesserae, as has been explained earlier. Becatti also reminds us that the refined emblematic designs and polychromatic pieces of the late Republican period are missing at Ostia; this is understandable in view of the high cost of such work. The student can do no better than to refer to Becatti's text and study the detailed analysis of the various interpretations of techniques employed in relation to the writings of Pliny, Vitruvius and Varro; there for instance *lithostroton* is defined as a *pavimentum sectile* rather than as *pavimentum musivum* as Pliny has it.

In truth it seems that etymological analysis of the word *lithostroton* might produce the general meaning of 'pavement constructed with stones', which need not refer to technique or any special construction of the individual elements. The word 'stones' is generic and would apply equally to tesserae and to any other pieces of that material. But it is of significance that statistical analysis of the flooring at Ostia for the period from Sulla to Augustus shows that in the earliest dwellings there is a prevalence of *opus signinum* with *cocciopesto* of red, brown or white base, perhaps with a sober decoration of white tesserae or of *crustae* either irregularly or lozenge or square shaped. White and black tessellated mosaic begins in the time of Sulla with geometrical designs and a frugal repertory of motifs which includes plaiting, fine checkerboard patterns, hour-glass patterns, stepped triangles, rosettes with symmetrical petals and olive and heart-shaped leaves, and finally the buckler pattern. Beyond these special designs there are also various floral motifs – bunches of spiny acanthus with sinusoidal branches, scrolled vines ending in

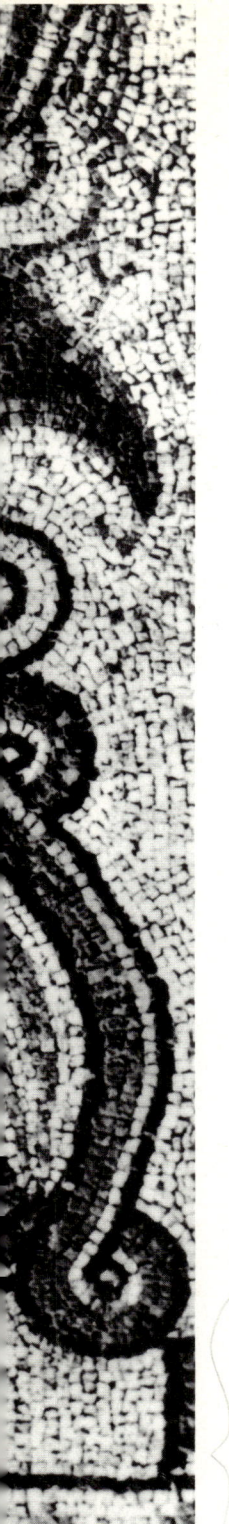

stylised leaves and buds, and small hooked vines with stylised twigs. . . .

The work is generally accurate, even if the designs are rather irregular. Throughout this period the use of tiny tesserae can be noted – always smaller than a centimetre in breadth – laid either horizontally or diagonally, a few rows being aligned parallel to the fillets and the design so as to create a break with the predominantly oblique tessellation of the background. The margins of the mosaic fields always have a white background; the black lines defining the borders are generally narrow, and the decorative elements rather small. Large black spaces are avoided.

Becatti also tells us that there exists at Ostia a series of mosaics which are less well documented, and which date from between the periods of Julius Claudius and Hadrian. It is noteworthy that from the first century the Romans developed a taste for small pictures of *opus sectile*, made polychromatically on a background of slate such as are found at Pompeii in the House of the Coloured Capitals. Similar pictures decorated with figures in hard stone were made again in the seventeenth and eighteenth centuries.

The periods of Hadrian and Antoninus were also periods of renewed activity in building at Ostia, and hence of a flowering of mosaic ornament, the *signinum* pavements going quite out of favour. At this time the decoration of the Imperial Palace which reflected the golden age of Rome was made; and even rooms for everyday use were given floral and figural mosaics, although invariably as pavement. The great hall of the Imperial Palace, for example, contained a polychrome geometric and flora floor, much finer than any of the others, and still betraying hellenistic influence. Illustrated here, however, is a mosaic which is a true masterpiece of its kind, and which is to be found in the Baths of Neptune (Plate 11). Sea nymphs alternate with Tritons, seahorses, fish and other marine animals with broad waving and curling tails. This grandiose design has a pictorial balance which is worthy of the most refined traditions of the art. The great value of mosaics at Ostia is that by studying their chronological evolution it is possible to trace the most important phases of development of the Roman *artum musivum*, even although the exact succession of the pieces may not always be clear. The prosperity and stability of the Severian period encouraged the development of both geometric motifs and figurative work. Styles are not invariably improved, however, for the ornate geometric patterns of the third century A.D. lack the earlier elegance and refinement, while figurative work is increasingly employed in the important areas of private residences. As the fifth century draws near one notices a slowing down in building activity. Restoration work now increasingly replaces the construction of new houses, and in the process the traditional black and white mosaics are replaced by a new taste for polychromatic figural pieces – one which reffects both the political and religious changes.

With the Edict of Constantine motifs inspired by Christianity appear, and throughout the late Imperial period it was the pleasing effects of polychrome which were sought at the expense of figural perfection; at the same time, pagan mosaic pavements were replaced by the decorations of the new churches of Christ. Indeed many of the mosaics at Ostia are more interesting as historical testimony than as works of art. Apart from those which we have examined in some detail, all the others tend to be extremely simple and it is evident from this that mosaic floors were popular because they were chea-

14 *Details of pavement mosaic from the cathedral at Aquileia.*

per and more durable than brick floors. Artists who produced their own work were rare, and the work was usually produced by workmen who repeated motifs that became coarse and even puerile with repetition. So while the taste for decorative form existed at Ostia, it was elsewhere during the same period that much finer work was being produced by artists who undertook the work in person.

After this mosaic was developed beyond its simple use as a method of paving, and became employed in the decoration of monuments, fountains, columns, and, finally of vaulting. The last century of the Republic saw the birth of the *opus musivum*, and by the second century A.D. provincial schools were established that continued the Hellenistic tradition. During the time of Hadrian, geometric decoration finally gave place to plant and polychromatic motifs, which, at first, were used in simple *emblemata*. Such designs acquired their own traditions, and so for example the *impluvium* of a house was most usually paved with marine or other aquatic motifs, often complete with fishing scenes and fish engaged in various activities. As has already been said, such pieces in their exposed position acquired special qualities of light and distinction when the rain fell upon them.

Hard stone was not much used yet, but vitreous pastes were quite widely employed, as they were in Greek work. So widespread was the use of mosaic in general by this period that an edict of Diocletian lays down the rates of payment for mosaicists. In the fourth century a *lapidarius structor*, a *calciscoctor* and the *musearius* all received the same wage which varied between 50 and 60 sesterces per day; the *pictor parietarius*, who was probably the equivalent of the modern house decorator, received 75 sesterces, while the *pictor imaginarius* earned no less than 175 sesterces. It is clear enough that at that time too the unfortunate mosaicist was poorly recompensed in comparison with the skilled decorator.[29]

Roman Domination

The progressive expansion of Roman dominion, even into African territory, produced few mosaic decorations in such provincial areas. These have in fact been found only in Carthage, apart from some tessellated monochrome incrustation work of *tesselatum* type in the House of the Cascade at Utica. Some pieces have been discovered at Cherchel, but these are earlier than the Flavian period.

With the Antonines (138–180 A.D.) there was considerable expansion in building activity, and mosaics were widely applied not only as pavement but also to vaulting, and there are the many fine examples from Ostia which have already been discussed, besides those in the Antonine Baths at Carthage and Hippo. Here too vegetal motifs were preferred as decoration, with acanthus leaves predominating, although animal pictures are also quite frequent.

Polychromatic decoration was in great evidence in geometric pattern work, and in animal and vegetal motifs during the third century A.D., especially in the provinces. Within Rome itself, decorations in black and white were more frequent.

Recently at Constanta on the Black Sea a large Roman gateway has been discovered, the date of which is uncertain, estimates varying between the third century A.D. and very much later periods. Above a series of large warehouses extends one of the finest mosaic pavements in our possession; about 600 square metres of it are still in good condition.

15   *Deer at a spring. Ravenna, mausoleum of Galla Placidia.*

16   *Interior of the mausoleum of Galla Placidia, Ravenna.*

Polychrome tesserae of calcareous stone and terracotta are used to depict geometric and vegetal motifs. In particular a large central circle enclosed in a rectangle contains motifs of vases, leaves and emblems which are woven into a design with a pleasing motif of cords and festoons. A border more than 6 metres wide runs round the room (Plates 12, 13).[30]

It is necessary to wait until the second half of the third century to discover a real transformation in design, and even then in the far flung Iberian provinces the black and white style persists. In the third and fourth centuries were developed the grandiose decorations of the Baths of Aquileia, Grado, and Piazza Armerina; and something of a revelation occurs with Circus Games in Germania and Gaul and mosaics at Reims, at Saint-Romain, the rustic calendar at Vienna and Lyons.[31]

Thus the *artum musivum*, once so dear to the Romans, becomes increasingly adopted generally and develops into polychrome especially during the period 235–285, finally assuming new strength in the period of Theodosius. By this time important examples occur throughout Europe, and in the Iberian Provinces at Barcelona and Madrid, with the villas of Tossa del Mar and Aletejo. In the two Gauls notable differences occur between the northern and southern parts, since in the former a Rhenish influence is at work while in the latter the influence of the Italian provinces – even of the few African examples – is felt.

In Austria the villas and baths were decorated with mosaics, and in Dalmatia there are the late (fourth and fifth century) mosaics of the Palace of Diocletian at Spalato, and of Salona near Spalato. The same period saw the making of mosaic work at Ephesus and at Baalbek and other works in Syria, Palestine and Mesopotamia such as that at the Villa of Constantine at Antioch.

Besides pavement mosaics it is possible to argue from evidence that mural mosaic is of very ancient origin and was probably used from the second century A.D. onwards. Known examples are: at Pompeii, the niche of the fountain at Zampillo; at Herculaneum, the pediment at the front part of a garden; at the baths and villa of Hadrian at Tivoli where there are traces of similar garden pieces of the third century. It is important to note how it was especially in this kind of mosaic that semi-precious stones were used to heighten the chromatic effect, lending tones that neither marble nor glass could give. Toesca[32] comments: 'Mural mosaics are closely related to painting since they have the same objective and in consequence they are not to be distinguished from one another as to treatment.'

Mosaics in Christian Art

Christian art seized early upon mosaics as an illustrative medium and used it extensively in churches from the first. Lavagnino[33] remarks in this connection:

'The Christians as they moved out of the catacombs into the churches sought to impart a monumental character to the latter, and so availed themselves of the technique of mosaic picture-making in which the subject gains prominence by shading.'

The rapid evolution of *tessellatum* in the paleo-Christian era was most certainly unpredictable; indeed the largest pieces of all date from that period. The very form that these works took presented considerable new problems. It was no longer a question simply of producing work upon a single flat plane.

17 *Tesserae mosaic. Ravenna, S. Vitale.*

18 *Overleaf left: The Emperor Justinian. Ravenna, S. Vitale.*

19 *Overleaf right: The Empress Theodora. Ravenna, S. Vitale.*

Now it was necessary to cover such areas as apses which offered surfaces with cylindrical and reversed curves, and, most difficult of all, hemispherical terminals; all these offered their own new problems of viewing perspective. Furthermore the sparse light provided by perhaps a single vertical loophole that was not uncommon in these early churches encouraged the use of a decorative medium which would gather and redistribute the light. As far as figural design is concerned, apse decoration was greatly enriched during the fourth century with the appearance in mosaic of the Apostles and saints, following upon the diffusion of their cults and relics. Here is an opposite phrase from Adolpho Venturi[34] upon the subject: 'In Italy, Rome shared its dominion in the art of mosaic with Ravenna, Venice and the towns of the lagoon; this formed part of the sacerdotal apparatus of the Church in the early centuries.'

Aquileia

Representations of the miraculous draught of fishes are common enough during the early centuries of Christianity; it is well known that, besides the evangelical reference, the symbol of the fish indicated Christ himself, from the letters of Greek word *Ictys* forming the initials of *Iesos Christos Theou Uios Soteer*, or 'Jesus Christ, Son of God, Saviour'.

For this reason the allusions to fish carrying this double message are numerous and varied in paleo-Christian art, and occur both in walls and pavements. It was in fact at the very beginning of the Christian Empire of Constantine that this predilection for aquatic scenes in the decoration of churches was most popular.

Preserved in the antique mosaic work of the cathedral at Aquileia is one of the most

eloquent and vast achievements of the early Christian era which was made during late Imperial times, when the city of Aquileia was still flourishing. The lively mosaic picture illustrated here (Plate 14) dates from the time of Bishop Theodorus; and more precisely from the period of the Council of Arles, at which he was present. We are thus in about the year 314. An inscription high on the right informs us that the work was undertaken with the help of the congregation. It is noticeable how, in the representation of this draught of fishes, pagan motifs intermingle with the symbols of the new faith, and how the winged children look more like Cupids than like the little angels they are supposed to represent.

In the case of the representation of Jonah and the whale, while it is clear that certain parts of the picture have been undertaken with great care, and that the colouring is often of fine quality, there is nonetheless a considerable difference between this work and that of the hellenistic Roman period discussed earlier. So far as style is concerned, the inconsistency in the mode of expression and the variety of manner with which the tesserae have been placed make it difficult to know whether the composition is the work of a single artist or of several. The mosaic is of the *tessellatum* variety; but, while the marine scene is made up of large, unequally disposed tesserae, the figures of the sprites are formed with small tesserae placed in rows with a certain predilection for verticality, as is to be seen clearly in the illustrated detail of the figure of the fishermna. From close examination of the various types of creatures – including the seabirds which are neither clearly in or out of the water, this would seem to be the work of minor artists who had probably seen similar composition elsewhere and wanted to reproduce them with more modest means. Ducati[35] is of the opinion that this rather confused work must have been composed by various hands since the harmony – which is considerable in some of the figures – is by no means consistent throughout.

The composition is not limited to a simple fishing scene, but is further decorated with animals and acanthus vines which are repeated in wide polychromatic borders and in octagonal shapes with symbolic motifs.

The general effect is stimulating and the whole constitutes a particularly pure expression of mosaic art of the fourth century. There are, however, a number of other fine works of the period which remained sufficiently intact to attract our interest and admiration, including some in Aquileia itself.

Ravenna

The very famous mosaics of the mausoleum of Galla Placidia at Ravenna (Plates 15, 16) date back to the year 430. They are extremely well preserved and consequently their structure may be studied closely.

The predominating background colour is an intense blue reminiscent of lapis lazuli, and this has the effect of making the figures stand out sharply, since these are of white or other light colours. The tesserae that form the *tessellatum* are almost entirely uniform in size, and the technique of fragmentation, common in *vermiculatum* work, is not used. The materials used are marble, vitreous pastes and gold. This last is not employed in large areas, but only in the clothes of the figures in relief, in order to light up some important feature, or to underline the figured cornices with Greek key-patterns or simple lines. Also in gold are the symbols of the evangelists and the stars of the cupola. But the artist has made much play with the angle of inclination of the tesserae and the reflection of the light that comes from small windows, veiled with thin pinky-yellow sheets of oriental alabaster so as to leave all in a mysterious half-light in which the glitter of the bright surfaces gives the illusion of perspective. The tendrils of acanthus interweaving pleasingly with the figures of the deer at the spring (Plate 15),

are lent plasticity by the brightness of the gold and by the shaded parts. Less in evidence is the lunette of the Good Shepherd above the entrance, since the whole is so enriched by the greens of the vegetation that the lunette is left too much in shadow; yet this is delicately made, and given a sense of movement by the tesserae. The whole work is Greek and Roman in feeling, yet made at a time of great artistic transformation.

In the majestic edifice of Sant' Apollinare Nuovo, some of the mosaic work dates from the time of Theodoric and some from the time of Bishop Agnello – that is, from the second half of the sixth century, when the church, which had formerly been Arian, passed to the Catholics. For this reason there are three clear divisions between the various pictorial episodes, which also differ as to the manner and style in which they are placed. The first is the large area between the arches and the windows; the second is the area of interval between the windows themselves; and the third occupies the space between the summit of the windows and the ceiling. These areas all have a well-defined theological function: they show the miracles of Christ, episodes from the Passion and the early Fathers of the Church and Prophets. Finally, on the left, a procession of twenty-two virgins (Plate 21) preceded by the three Magi (Plate 22) makes its way towards the enthroned Virgin Mary, while on the right a procession of twenty-six martyrs led by St Martin move towards Christ, also enthroned.

The processions of virgins and martyrs are some decades later than the rest. Stylistically the mosaics dating from the time of Theodoric show signs of Greco-Roman influence, while those dating from the time of Bishop Agnello are typically Byzantine.[36] The pieces have been much restored and altered since

43

21 *The Virgins' Procession. Ravenna, S. Apollinare Nuovo.*

22 *Detail of one of the three Kings. Ravenna, S. Apollinare Nuovo.*

the church was changed to the Catholic cult, but concept and form remain to reveal the artistic taste and manner of the Byzantine era, when it was usual to value more highly the movement of masses rather than the individual expressions of the figures, which are fixed and practically identical. Most striking is the contrast between the splendour of the gold background and the purity of the robes of the figures: the martyrs are dressed soberly, and the virgins given embroidery and gems. The red fruit of the stylised vegetation is prominent, while the meadow is of a most delicate green. The richness of colour of the figures of the Magi is also striking, although it is true that these figures have been much restored and in part re-made. All the tesserae used in these mosaics are small, quadrangular and of marble or vitreous paste.

The mosaics of San Vitale (Plates 17, 18, 19, 20) were executed between 546 and 548. Lavagnino[37] suggests: 'It is not impossible that mosaicists were sent from Byzantium itself to the church in Ravenna, in order to undertake the stone portraits of the Augustans.' These portraits are indeed of stone; not only because they are mosaics, but also because of the stony fixity of their gaze and the immobility of their richly-clothed figures.

The apse of this wonderful building glows with the colour and brilliance of the tesserae that illuminate it. It is a triumph of gold, gems and precious materials. Everything glitters from capitals to arches, from the lunettes to the bowl-shaped vault with the Theophany. Theodora with her retinue and Justinian, Emperor of the East (Plates 18, 19), with his cloak and great fibula, are majestically imperial.

As has already been remarked the tesserae are, with rare exceptions, of practically uniform size and quadrangular in shape. In the series of episodes, most outstanding are the representations of the sacrifices of Abel, Melchizedec, and Isaac. Also very fine are the Hospitality of Abraham and the faces of Christ, his Apostles, and Saints Gervasius and Protasius in the triumphal arch. Here, too, the mural mosaics have a didactic function and are used to encourage the faithful to meditation upon the mysteries of the faith.

We are far indeed from the Roman paving mosaics of Ostia – those typical expressions of a comfortable life that seek to recall the excitement of the sea for those who refresh themselves in their private swimming pools. Here, on the other hand, the mosaics are a hymn to the new faith that has left cold symbolism far behind to reveal with human images the sublime presence exalted in the preciousness of the material. This material was chosen with care and skill, not by contractors accustomed to meet their clients' wishes with patterns repeated *ad infinitum*, but by artists, secure in their knowledge of the sacred books, whose joy it was to illustrate the mysteries of their faith.

The almost inexhaustible Ravenna series continues with the Baptistry of the Cathedral, the Baptistry of the Arians and the Archiepiscopal chapel.

The Ravenna mosaics of the fifth and sixth centuries are unique in that they combine harmoniously Roman, Barbarian, and Oriental influences. The ostentatious art of the East is assimilated with the Latin tradition, and thus there is developed at Ravenna a local school of mosaic that represents a new departure, different from the work of any other school.

Also at Ravenna, while the presbytery at San Vitale was being completed in 549, a new church, Sant'Apollinare in Classe, was consecrated which contained mosaic work in

the absidal area (Plate 23). Of firmly Byzantine inspiration, it is one of the finest churches in the city. Beneath the great cross which dominates the whole composition of the apse, sits enthroned the figure of St Apollinare, first Bishop of Ravenna. He is dressed in his sacred robes and is flanked by twelve little sheep, six on each side, who represent the faithful in the care of the Holy Shepherd.

This is the last mosaic at Ravenna which shows directly the influence of Byzantium. It has connections with the apse in the Cathedral of Parenzo which dates from the second half of the fourth century, and where there

23 *St Matthew (detail). Ravenna, S. Apollinare in Classe.*

24 *Overleaf: The Last Supper. Thirteenth-century mosaic. Venice, S. Marco.*

are representations of the Virgin enthroned with the Child on her knees, attended by two angels and three saints who offer crowns. The rotonda of St George at Salonika, built in the time of Theodoric, is decorated with similar mosaics.

Many mosaics which have been described at Ravenna have subsequently been lost. Such were those in the ancient Cathedral of Ursia,[39] the basilica of St Peter in Classe, and the churches of San Giovanni Evangelista, Santa Croce, Santa Maria Maggiore, and Sant' Agata.

Venice

In Venice the mosaics of San Marco must certainly have pride of place. Of them P. Toesca, and F. Forlati[38] write as follows: 'The most ancient of the mosaics of San Marco are the finest objects in the golden basilica, and remain in the mind's eye almost mysteriously.'

These mosaics have a certain connection with Byzantine work, especially that during the period between the eleventh and fourteenth centuries. All however, are vividly polychrome and whole fields of gold serve to enhance their splendour (Plate 24). Toesca and Forlati[39] discuss the technique as follows:

'We should like finally to record certain facts concerning the technique of ancient mosaics. It was established for the first time that the mosaicists, having executed in the first stratum of plaster 'a scaletti' or 'a bozzette' initial designs (the famous *sinopie*) such as are found also at Ravenna and Monreale, produced in all colours of plaster composed of marble and dust and lime stone, the scene that the mosaicist and his helpers would then translate into mosaic while the plaster was still wet.

'We thus have a fresco which would immediately be given permanence in the form of a mantle of marble and enamel tesserae.'

It is clear that during that highly productive period of mosaic making there existed a technique which could permit mosaics to be made spontaneously; and it was not until later that more highly organised systems led to decadence. In the neighbourhood of Venice, Byzantine influence is to be noted clearly in the twelfth-century mosaics of Santa Maria e Donato at Murano, and in the absidal mosaics in the Chapel of the Sacrament in the cathedral at Torcello.

So far as the evolution of style is concerned – an important aspect of the present study – Lavagnino[40] comments at length on thirteenth-century Venice, where Byzantine forms still appeared albeit with a reduction in 'expressionist terms'; such was the prelude to the new academy, which would encourage 'a violent and contorted manner of representation, together with endless superficial stylisations, contrived gestures, and violent slashes of colour.'

Certainly in this magnificent 'golden basilica' one senses certain marked similarities to the churches of Sicily. Here, too, the immensity of the golden backgrounds fill one with admiration. As has already been suggested, there is inevitably a diversity of form and a difference of manner which has caused uncertainty among those critics who have entered the arguments that surround researches into these mosaics. These are mosaics both ancient and modern; above all, however, numerous restorations have significantly modified both effects of light and forms.

Toesca and Forlati are particularly useful in this respect since they produce factual evidence concerning restorations as follows:[41] 'In San Marco the Procurators recommended

25 *Finding of the relics of St Mark. Venice, S. Marco.*

the restorers to give their attention to the iconography of the mosaics which were to be restored or renewed. However, many of the ancient pictures and their original order were disarranged or lost. In the apse the large Christ enthroned has replaced (1506) the Pantocrator, which originally certainly must have resembled the Byzantine mosaics of San Luca in Folcide, of Daphni, Cefalu and Monreale. If the cycle of Great Feasts was ever shown in sequence, as in the enamels of the "Pala d'oro", it is now fragmentary and divided up. Furthermore, strange and repetitive incidents were introduced into the story of the Patron Apostle and of the transporting of his relics to the church.'

After these initial criticisms the authors examine minutely all the mosaics, and in particular note the Byzantine iconographic composition of the three main cupolas in the principal apse of San Marco. They mention that besides vitreous pastes many varieties of marble are used in the mosaic surfaces. These, it seems, were sent from Constantinople itself by order of the Doge Enrico Dandolo.

Many of the figures, however, seem more carelessly made than the Sicilian ones, both as to the size of the tesserae and as to their placing. The composition of the pictures themselves also seems lacking in care, as in the group of bearers which figure in the story from Genesis in the porch.

On the other hand the scenes from the story of the removal and transport of the Relics from Alexandria (Plate 25) show much more careful handling; the tesserae are smaller and the result is correspondingly more pleasing. There is no need to remark much upon the state of conservation of these pieces, since Toesca and Forlati mention not only that they are restored antiques but that time has produced further gaps in the tesserae. They write:[42] 'The mosaic of two angels on the door of the treasury seems posterior to 1231; that on the door to the left of the porch of the Basilica representing the four bronze horses taken in 1205 from Constantinople and placed some years later on the façade, is certainly before 1275. Finally, the mosaics of the Baptistry are certainly of the time of Andrea Dandolo (1342–1354), while in 1355 the Chapel of Sant' Isidoro, begun by the same Dandolo, was completed.'

Toesca and Forlati further mention that the mosaics of the stories of the Madonna and the Childhood of Christ have been rather grossly reconstructed.

The authors distinguish between the work of masters and of ordinary craftsmen at San Marco. The 'Master of the Temptations of Christ' in the arch towards the right transept followed the scheme of the Palatine Chapel and of the Daphni mosaic, and the work is thus of Byzantine inspiration. The 'Master of the Ascension' in the central cupola also has Byzantine themes, although there are differences with the preceding piece. To the same artist are attributed the mosaics of the passion of Christ in the neighbouring arch. Toesca and Forlati deduce by comparing with them the mosaics of San Paolo at Rome, made by artists brought from Venice, that the San Marco mosaics must belong to the latter part of the twelfth century or to the beginning of the thirteenth. Another masterpiece is the 'Agony in the Garden' which has the feeling of Byzantine work that belonged to the 'Master of Icons'. This manner seeks effects in the ornament and colour of the background which give prominence to figures that are attenuated in a rather moderate Byzantine fashion. This master probably worked at the beginning of the thirteenth century. Toesca, in his detailed analysis, suggests that 'the

26 *Ceiling and cupola of the Baptistery of S. Giovanni, Florence.*

27 *Mosaic capital from the great arch of the presbytery. Florence, Baptistery of S. Giovanni.*

artist who produced the work in the porch seems to have begun his task at the beginning of the thirteenth century'. The external mosaic over the left-hand door of the porch was presumably completed before 1275. The Doge Andrea Dandolo ordered the mosaics of the Baptistery of San Marco, which show a late Byzantine style. We are thus halfway through the fourteenth century and in both the culture and art of Venice there are clear signs of new influence initiated by Paolo da Venezia, whose modernist ideas exercised strong effect. Mosaic work which for centuries had triumphed by employing the forms, manners and spirit of Byzantium, finally had to succumb to a decadence that had already established itself elsewhere in Italy.

The foregoing remarks on the mosaics of San Marco and the comparisons with Sicilian work with which there are so many points of contact, should help to give some idea of this important but brief phase of artistic achievement. The technique followed is almost uniformly that of *tessellatum*, and in spite of the fact that some areas of the works display very small tesserae, the backgrounds, ornaments and robes have quite large tesserae which are of generally constant size. It is certainly true that the numerous restorations and intrusions can only serve to confuse the observer.

Subsequently the master mosaicists transferred from Venice to Rome and Florence at the end of the thirteenth century, where pictures on canvas and wood and fresco painting prevailed, especially in Tuscany. As a parallel development in the north, and first of all in Milan, during the first half of the fifth century, appeared the mosaics of Sant'Aquilino which is a part of San Lorenzo, and those of the church of San Vittore in Ciel d'Oro near Sant'Ambrogio.

Tuscany

In Tuscany among those mosaics of which students have tried to identify the artist, perhaps the greatest is the cycle of figures in the Baptistery of San Giovanni at Florence (Plate 26).[43] Giorgio Vasari insists that these are the work of Apollonius who was supposed to be Greek and of his Florentine student Andrea Tafi. Toesca on the other hand proposes to attribute some parts to Cimabue and his school, comparing the work to the figure of the Evangelist in the cathedral at Pisa. It is further suggested that an inscription in the mosaic on the vault of the apse indicates that the work was begun in May 1225 by the Franciscan Jacopo Torrita, called 'Fra Mino', and was perhaps completed during the third decade of the following century. Paatz[44] cites other authors, among them Galdo Gaddi. The most important cycle in these mosaics covers the octagonal cupola and ends towards the apse with a large representation of the Redeemer. Starting from the base of the cupola, patriarchs, prophets, deacons and bishops are to be observed. The arch of

28 Mosaic decorating the cupola of the Baptistery of S. Giovanni.

the *scarsella* is amply decorated and it seems that the whole work may have been begun from this point by the hand of the abovementioned Franciscan Jacopo. It is not known precisely which parts are his work and which the work of his collaborators, but the disposition of the figures and the greater spacing that is used in this arch in comparison with the crowded representation of the cupola suggest that the former may be the work of the master. Some would see Venetian influence in this work, while others suggest Roman influence; it is certainly difficult to identify a single personality as the author of these pieces.

Pictorial composition is carefully studied and the large figure of John the Baptist, which corresponds to that of the Virgin Mary on the other side, is flanked by grandiose capitals decorated with acanthus vines in various shaded colours that stand out from a vast background of gold (Plate 27). From the top of these, genuflecting figures support a vast *tondo*, very finely designed with eight figures, symbolic Christian signs, and deer, the latter drinking from water that pours from sumptuous vases. The eight polychrome figures are those of Abraham, Moses, Isaiah, Jeremiah, Ezechiel, Daniel, Jacob and Isaac. They encircle the mystical haloed lamb. This part of the mosaic of the Baptistery is noticeably different from all the rest of the cupola, both as to its geometrical design and clear presentation, and as to the sense of colour and shading which suggests a special talent. The division of the figures within the tondo is more Roman than Venetian in feeling and the general decorative effect places them at an enormous distance from the other scenes in the same building. Above all, the technique is different: the tesserae are disposed regularly with an almost academic meticulousness, and the outlines of the borders of the central circle are not differentiated from one another. There are a few very obvious areas of restoration, but what remains of the original may be safely attributed to Fra Jacopo.

The incidents pictured on the cupola are arranged at various levels marked by horizontal lines. Starting from the top there are first of all various ornamentations (Plate 28). These are followed by Christ surrounded by angels, stories from Genesis, the story of Joseph, episodes from the life of Christ and finally the story of the life of the Baptist himself.

All these mosaics date from the first part of the thirteenth century and are attributed generally to Venetian masters. It is thought that they worked from cartoons furnished by the Florentines, among whom would be the so-called 'Maestro della Maddalena'. It has already been mentioned that there was a great diversity between these scenes and the scenes on the arch of the *scarsella*. There have been many restorations which began during the period between 1343 and 1412 with the work of Zaccaria d'Andrea, Filippo di Corso, and Donato di Donato.[45]

Further restorations were made by Baldovinetti at the end of the fifteenth century. Repairs were made in various ways, some with painted tesserae. It has been suggested that between 1898 and 1907 'the Murder of Cain', 'the appearance of the Almighty to Noah', and 'the Building of the Ark' were entirely replaced. It was during this period that the work on the cathedral at Florence was undertaken and we learn from de Witt[46] how massive these restorations were, above all those made by the Opificio delle Pietre Dure[47] (the Florentine workshop where hard stones were worked) under the direction of Marchionni and Orlandini up to 1940. It is easy to understand how these efforts hindered re-

29 *Bowl-shaped vault in the apse. Basilica of S. Miniato al Monte.*

search. Difficulties of attribution for these reasons have always existed. We ourselves have analysed the technique of various areas of decoration and there is no doubt that each cycle has been treated differently from the others, not only in that there is a difference in figurative conception, but also in that different materials have been used and in different ways. All this seems to confirm the hypothesis that the decoration has been the work of artists of various schools.

In the stories of the life of the Baptist, the pattern in which the tesserae are laid is both minute and regular in all the various episodes. The vegetation is stylised everywhere and vitreous pastes are largely used to give gentle shaded colours. All this differs entirely from the mosaics of the *scarsella* which we have already discussed. Similar technical treatment is observable in the Christological illustrations.

In these, the expressions on the faces, the draperies and gestures, even if they show Venetian influence with some Hellenistic and Byzantine overtones, have a certain personal touch which clearly shows how these tendencies of style were given a Tuscan flavour to be noted in so many other fields of art, including architecture. Leading critics, both contemporary and of the past, have been unable to make a specific attribution for these works. It is hard to agree with the attempt to see in them the hand of Cimabue and even Giotto, as has been suggested. Even de Witt is much perplexed by the continual intervention of restorers who, for him, have cancelled the authenticity of the pieces. These restorations are undertaken so easily in the case of mosaic work, partly because it is so much easier to add pieces of marble or vitreous pastes than it is to restore an oil painting or a fresco. The truth is, however, that good restoration is no easier for mosaics than for any other art work. In mosaics, as in painting, sculpture and architecture, there are personal characteristics which are practically impossible to copy just, as those in handwriting have made it almost impervious to forgery.

It is usually possible to recognise the manner and taste of any period in mosaic work by reference to certain particulars, often structural ones, even if it is impossible to name the individual artist. Such particulars relate not only to the tesserae themselves, the manner in which they were cut and placed, but also to the cements which were used – whether they were made simply from lime, to which might be added sand, pumice, *cocciopesto*, and marble dust, or whether hot or cold gum mastic was used. Where the restorer takes no account of

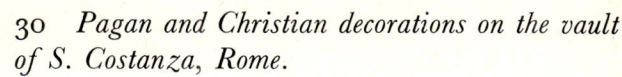

30 *Pagan and Christian decorations on the vault of S. Costanza, Rome.*

these factors, and where he decides to fill gaps from his imagination without regard to historical accuracy, he certainly does not make any contribution to research. In the Florentine Baptistery and elsewhere the repairs were all undertaken on a very large scale, even at the cost of completely remaking anything that had been damaged by time, so that any student who wishes to decide upon an attribution of the original must take account of the complexity of these successive restorations which may falsify even technical research.

Stories from Genesis and the story of Joseph differ from preceding works in personality and in the expressions of the faces and the postures. The figure of Christ is conferring a blessing in the Byzantine manner with thumb and fourth finger united; the multiplicity of the figures sometimes forces them against one another; the animals enter the ark in a dense crowd; all these things mark the differences with the previous works. In some pictures the disposition and form of the tesserae themselves are quite different. The Last Judgement is different again. The folds of the gowns, the angle of the faces and the cut of the beards give the work a Greek character. The wings of the angels and the forms of the vegetation are different too. The colours are more lively. In certain areas the work is no longer even of the *tessellatum* kind, but rather of *vermiculatum*, which suggests direct intervention of the master artist. Characteristic in this respect is the group of the three patriarchs which is of the finest workmanship and very different from large parts of the other pictures. The careful shading of the face of the Redeemer in the great *tondo* recalls similar figures from Sicily, while the brilliant and highly varied colouring of the leading figures and of the minute details which requires fragmentation of the tesserae

59

31 *Fourth-century mosaic. Rome, S. Costanza.*

suggests Venetian mosaic. De Witt[48] writes: 'It seems ungrateful to forget the makers of this masterpiece which contributes so largely to the brilliant unity of the edifice and represents one of the most remarkable contributions to the tradition of mosaic at a time when creative imagination was in decay. The achievement is to be all the more highly prized because it occurred in a Florentine or Tuscan environment where this method of mural representation was undertaken by workers who were not trained in it, as they had been for centuries in the practice of other related arts'. All the critics are agreed however that the Florentines, wishing to enhance the name of their Baptistry, decided upon the use of mosaic which could contribute so thoroughly to the feeling of majesty pervading this splendid monument, and which could withstand the ravages of time so much more effectively than other media. The restorers too undertook their labours with the same intention and it seems to be true that Florentines of every era have been filled with the profound wish to conserve their works of art by any means at their disposal. The Baptistry is unique in the history of art and its mosaics deserve to be a special object of study. It is remarkable how, in this single step, an illustrative system of such vast proportions was introduced to Florence and undertaken in a manner unequalled in any other monument in the city.

Another notable monument is the great absidal mosaic of San Miniato al Monte (Plate 29) which dates from 1297. Although it is restored, this grandiose mosaic with the golden background has characteristics that cannot be overlooked. It shows obvious influence from Greece and Byzantium. Christ Pantocrator is seated on a sumptuous throne flanked by the Virgin and the titular saint of the church, San Miniato, whom he is crowning King of Armenia. Below the figures, the symbols of the four Evangelists complete this picture with great richness of colour. The design is minutely worked, and the figures are realistic and dressed in the richest of garments enhanced with gold. The vegetation on the other hand is pleasingly stylised and realised with great imagination, with symbolic animals vaguely suggested. Almost the whole of the composition is obtained by the use of vitreous pastes which shine brightly and give a slightly uneven surface, the angle of the tesserae being variously altered. There is a wide gradation of colours with all the tones of green, red, grey, blue and gold. The name of the artist is unknown, but he was certainly an artist of considerable importance who has infused into this apse both his rich theological knowledge and his skill as a mosaicist. We are now at the end of the thirteenth century and already in Florence can be seen the works of great artists who have shaken the foundations of mosaic art by the novelty of their compositions which brought about a true artistic revaluation.

Thus mosaic scenes were now filled with figures and designs which did not leave a single corner empty. Where nothing else could be done, an inscription was added which might add to the didactic effect of the narrative.

Also intricately decorated is the whole internal façade of the intrados of the arch, in which the polychrome figures of the saints on a gold background alternate with vines, birds and the heads of winged and haloed angels. Immediately above the head of Christ – who has a crossed halo ornamented with four hemispheres of glass – is placed in a small *tondo* the figure of the Holy Ghost in the form of a white dove. The whole is inserted in the

grandiose cornice of green and white marble intarsio surrounding the windows, through which filters a tenuous light veiled by a sheet of oriental alabaster which becomes pink as the sun rises. Here, architecture and mosaic have been composed in relation to each other and the effect of one complements that of the other. We should like to point out that, as a complement to architecture, mosaic work has quite a different value from fresco, tempera or encaustic work. Mosaic forms part of the surface which carries it, and perhaps

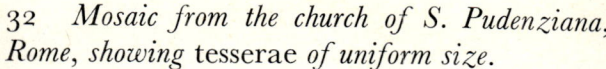

32 *Mosaic from the church of S. Pudenziana, Rome, showing* tesserae *of uniform size.*

for this reason has an expressive power more suitable to the monumental complex than other media of decoration.

Other important mosaics in Tuscany are to be found in Pisa Cathedral[49] and at Lucca. It is interesting to observe that while Byzantine influence is certainly present in all these works, there is also a local influence which may be described as a mixture of gothic and romanesque traditions.

Rome

Among the oldest post-Ravenna mosaics in Rome, the most important are those of the Basilica of Santa Costanza, those of Santa Pudenziana and those of the nave of Santa Maria Maggiore (fifth century).[50] Perhaps the earliest example of all, dating from the fourth century, is the famous and elegant consruction of Santa Costanza, built on a circular plan near to Sant'Agnese in the Via Nomentana. This example shows once again how mosaic – essentially a pagan art – was transformed in order to adapt itself to the demands of the Christian Church, often, however, keeping the same pagan designs. The mural decorations of this monument show pagan characteristics in their white background – so common in ancient Roman paving – and also in the choice of subjects among which figure cupids, birds, cornucopias, mirrors, carts pulled by oxen, all intermingling with Christian symbols (Plates 30, 31). At first glance one has the impression that the edifice had initially been a temple of Bacchus and had only later, for some unknown reason, become adapted to other functions. Until the seventeenth century it was not in fact a sacred place, and served as a reunion hall for Dutch painters. In Santa Pudenziana (Plate 32) near the Piazza del Esquilino on the Via Urbana there are rather later mosaics, dating from the very end of the fourth century, although they were altered and restored in the sixteenth century. They contain obviously Christian motifs with no trace of pagan influence. They are quite different in manner

33 *Angel on the vault of the chapel of S. Zenone. Rome, S. Prassede.*

from those in Santa Costanza. According to Lavagnino[51] they are to be dated between 384 and 398. Other students place them rather between 402 and 417. It is interesting to observe how, even though the works have been subject to much restoration, their essential character provides a clear view of the use of mosaic in these first centuries of the Christian era, and shows how successfully these early artists dealt with difficult subjects. The large mosaic which occupies the whole of the top part of the apse is classified as Hellenistic-Roman by Lavagnino, It depicts Christ triumphant and enthroned in the presence of St Praxides and St Pudenziana. These two were sisters, daughters of the Senator Pudenzio who received St Peter himself in his home. They were baptised with their father by the Apostle, together with their brothers Novatus and Timothy, and their ninety servants. Both sisters were martyrized and the house they lived in was consecrated by Pope Pius I, in about the middle of the second century. It thus became a church, and after undergoing various transformations between the fourth and eighth centuries, it is now as it was left by Cardinal Gaetani in 1598. The absidal mosaic is dated and seeks to express the admiration of the faithful for these two saints who are placed in prominent positions in respect to all the other figures. In the upper part of the wall the four large symbols of the Evangelists dominate the mosaic, and the cross stands out in triumph amongst numerous pagan temples. Christ blessing is seated on a throne surrounded by St Pudenziana holding the martyr's crown above the head of St Paul, and St Praxides in the same attitude in relation to St Peter, next to whom is the Senator Pudenzio (Plate 32); various other figures complete the scene amongst whom are perhaps Novatus and Timothy. The importance of this example is that it can serve as the most ancient standard of comparison by which may be judged various later pieces, both as to their style and execution. The earliest Christian art has left here a most important testimony, one which has been much studied in the past and which has always been compared to the many other mosaics in Roman churches. In it the figures give the sensation of not being all on one plane, but shown in perspective, and each one of them has an expression of its own – a very different thing from the uniform masks which are so often found in work of this period. Lavagnino distinguishes in them a specific Roman style and this certainly seems to be justified.

Matthiae[52] writes: 'The mosaicist of Santa Puzenziana was without doubt a great master. This is to be deduced from the fine concreteness of the vision, from the balance of the composition, from the psychological precision with which each character is defined, and from the colours and vigour of the sentiment transmitted by the work.' In his remarkable book, this great scholar analyses and illustrates all the mosaics in the churches of Rome. From it we have made a list, with essential dates. It is interesting that, in Rome, mosaic was widespread in churches great and small a very long time before painting became popular. Thus in Santa Sabina there are remains of decorations dating from the fifth century, although only on the walls of the entrance; in the Lateran Baptistery there are mosaics of the sixth century, in the Basilica of San Paolo at Ostia the triumphal arch has work dating between 440 and 450; the ancient decoration of St Peter's was restored by Gregory IX (1227–1241); the mosaics of Sant'Agata dei Goti and of Sant'Andrea in Catabarbara are lost (the first was executed between 470 and 472); the church of San

34 *Absidal mosaic. Rome, S. Agnese.*

35 *Absidal mosaic. Rome, S. Clemente.*

Teodoro has a mosaic decoration which comes from a slightly later phase than that at Santi Cosma e Damiano; 'in San Lorenzo reconstructed by Pelagius II (559–579) there remains only the mosaic of the arch with the Redeemer seated in the globe between Peter and Paul, the deacons Stefano and Lorenzo, the priest Ippolito and the Pope, all these figures standing out on the gold background' (Plate 37); Sant'Agnese reconstructed by Honorius I (625–638), over the tomb of the martyr St Agnes, was decorated with an absidal mosaic (Plate 34); in Santo Stefano Rotondo 'there are the remains of a mosaic in a radial chapel, not contemporary with the rest of the building, but added by Pope Theodorus (642–649)'; San Venanzio was also decorated by Theodorus with an absidal mosaic which goes back to the time of Pope Agatho (678–682); the mosaic in the arch of the church of Santi Cosma e Damiano may according to Matthiae date back to the time of Pope Sergius I (687–701), while that of the *catino* is certainly by a different hand: 'Pope John VII (705–707) erected in old St Peter's an oratory dedicated to the Virgin Mary and decorated it with mosaics that were destroyed in 1606 and were replaced by simple sketches.'

'In the Vatican crypt is preserved a mosaic which, according to a tradition that there is no reason to doubt, decorated the tomb of Otto II who died at Rome in the year 983 and was buried in the atrium of the old church.' The Basilica of San Clemente, reconstructed at the beginning of the twelfth century and consecrated probably in 1218, keeps almost unchanged the mosaics of the apse and the arch (Plate 35); the Trasteverine church dedicated to the Virgin Mary which, according to tradition, was built on the spot where a fountain of oil flowed on the morning of the nativity, was reconstructed by Pope Vincenzo II (1130–1143) and decorated with mosaics. In the *catino* of the apse and in the arch that encloses it in Santa Maria Nuova in the Roman Forum, there remains only the absidal *catino* decorated in mosaic, which is normally considered a work of the second half of the twelfth century; decorated also with mosaic were the apse and triumphal arch of old St Peter's; the most important document of medieval mosaic in the apse of San Paolo is the letter sent by Pope Honorius III on 23 January 1218 to the Doge of Venice asking for the help of two more mosaicists in addition to those who were already working on the mosaic of the church at Ostia, the work of which was evidently going too slowly.

The façade of San Paolo fuori le Mura was ornamented with mosaics commissioned by Pope John XXII (1316–1334) and undertaken by the same artist.[53]

In Santa Maria Maggiore, the thirty-six mosaics which are to be found above the triumphal arch and which lead right down the nave have a grandeur which shows classical influence and have been the subject of much uncertainty and discussion. Some students have ascribed them to the papacy of Sixtus III (432–440),[54] while others attribute them to the fourth century and others again place those of the nave and those of the triumphal arch in the fifth century. Other attributions have been made which would place the mosaics of the nave earlier still, before the fourth century and anterior to Pope Liberius (352–361) and suggest that this is the work of Hellenistic artists. 'But it seems, however, that the two groups of mosaics are contemporary with the fifth century and that those framed in the lateral walls are derived from some ancient Hellenistic prototypes. Furthermore it is interesting that the Hellenis-

SCA AGNES

36 *Mosaic of the chapel of S. Zenone. Rome, S. Prassede.*

37 *Absidal mosaic. Rome, S. Lorenzo fuori le Mura.*

38 *Overleaf: The Coronation of the Virgin by Torriti. Apse of S. Maria Maggiore, Rome.*

tic motifs have been interpreted with a mosaic technique which seeks to imitate painting in its shading, in the gently graded colours, and in the softly indicated lines; and that the mosaicists of the triumphal arch had before them more modern designs, and interpreted them with a more livelier and bolder technique which was perfectly adapted to its purpose and which produced effects very different from mosaics imitating fresco painting. These are precisely the intentions of the mosaicists of the lateral walls.'[55]

Two great mosaicists, Torriti and Cavallini, have left fine work which is still to be seen. Jacopo Torriti is an important figure in fourteenth-century Rome, although his importance is limited now by the few works of his hand that have survived. He, together with Jacopo Da Camerino, began the great absidal mosaic in San Giovanni in Laterano under Nicholas IV (1288-1294) and finished it at the beginning of the following century. Later, after 1307, were completed seven compositions between the windows at the base of the vaulting. These were the Purification of St Anne, mother of the Virgin Mary, the Annunciation, the Nativity, the Death of the Virgin Mary, the Adoration of the Magi, the Purification of Mary and Simon.[56] The mosaic was completely destroyed and remade between 1875 and 1876 and the only work which is certainly by Torriti in Rome is the absidal mosaic of Santa Maria Maggiore (Plate 38). Its figures, as Lavagnino suggests,[57] are disposed according to the academic principles of the Byzanto-Venetian school 'with slits of light in the centre of each fold'. But it is a rather solemn composition which has lost much of the spirit of the ancient mosaicists by trying to approach too closely the themes which are more commonly depicted in fresco painting.

Pietro Cavallini[58] was a contemporary of Torriti and of his work remain a large number of undoubtedly original pieces. He was both a painter and a sculptor and his mosaic work reveals his taste for fresco. Matthiae writes: 'Although Cavallini's work is of high quality he does not use mosaic with the understanding that its special possibilities deserve. He uses it as if it were fresco painting.'[59] We learn from Lavagnino[60] that in 1273 he signed his name to a legal document as that of an ancient Roman family – 'Pietro detto Cavallini dei Cerroni'. Thus it is clear that Cavallini was an added name. His mosaics in Santa Maria in Trastevere (Plate 39) are dated 1291 and the façade of the Ostia Basilica was decorated with mosaics by him at the behest of Pope John XXII (1316-1334). His life was a long one for he was born between 1240 and 1250 and he probably died between 1340 and 1350. It is possible to attribute to him with certainty the mosaics of the façade below the absidal *semi-catino* of Santa Maria in Trastevere which consists of six pictures showing scenes from the life of the Virgin together with a central scene showing the apotheosis of the Virgin between St Peter and St Paul. When one compares the work of this artist with that of Torriti in Santa Maria Maggiore, one finds an identical background of training.[61] In Cavallini also is to be observed a tendency towards Hellenistic style which is a result of Roman influence, and his considerable artistic personality is noticeable in his mosaic work. These 'mosaic paintings' have been related by Lavagnino to the Byzantine tradition, although the artist never uses oriental style without the stamp of his own personality. A relationship with Giotto has also been suggested and Gerspach even goes so far as to make Cavallini the former's pupil;[62] but it is certain that Cavallini

✝ GENTIBVS IGNOTVS STELLA DVCE NOSCITV[R]
IN PRESEPE IACENS CELI TERREQ: PROFVNDI
CONDITOR · ATQ: MAGI MYRRAM THVS AC[C]

39 *The Adoration of the Magi, by Cavallini. Rome, S. Maria in Trastevere.*

acquired fame both as a painter and as a mosaicist. Nonetheless, this tendency to treat mosaic as though it was fresco painting marks the beginning of a decadence of mosaic art which was forced eventually to submit to the powerful will of the Tuscan painters, foremost among whom was Giotto himself who left a great testimony to the art of mosaics. Matthiae (page 391, *op. cit.*) writes: 'The great period of medieval Roman mosaics closes with the "Navicella" of Giotto over the entrance of the Vatican Basilica.' This mosaic over which there has been so much controversy was placed on the walls of the entrance, removed in 1610, restored and completed by Marcello Provenzale in 1618, and replaced in the entrance of the Vatican palace. It was taken down once more and further restored in 1675 by Vincenzo Manenti and thus completely differs from the original, even as to the general lines of the composition. The only evidence of the pictorial manner Giotto used to illustrate great themes of his mosaic, inspired by the writings of Matthew (14: 22-29) (Matthiae, *op. cit.*, p. 392) that remains are the two angels that were found, one in the Vatican crypt in 1727, and the other in San Pietro Ispano at Boville Ernica in 1612 (Plate 40). There is controversy over the authorship of these two, especially in view of the fact that they were found so far apart. Matthiae writes (p. 393): 'The thousand-year-old experience and techniques of the great mosaicists were interpreted freshly by Cavallini who was intent on obtaining the effects of fresco in mosaic work. His pictorial technique with its highlights and rapid touches remains that of a painter. He risks a great deal to adapt the techniques of fresco to mosaics without making the results look unnatural. He successfully meets the demands of his objectives without allowing them to

overwhelm him.' These remarks sum up most effectively the concepts of 'painting in mosaics' and show clearly how fine effects can be obtained provided that the artist does not make concessions to rules that apply only in other fields. But the golden age of medieval mosaics was over, even if there are occasionally fine works from later artists. Filippo Rusuti is considered a follower of Cavallini; only one work of his is recognised with certainty, part of the decoration in the façade of Santa Maria Maggiore. With the beginning of the Renaissance, after the supreme efforts in San Marco at Venice and in St Peter's at Rome,[63] mosaic work was superseded by painting.

Sicily

As we have seen, the art of mosaics was exported from Byzantium and took root and developed in various local schools. In Italy in the twelfth century, partly as a result of political influence and foreign domination, there was a remarkable flowering of specifically regional work, among which the Sicilian

40 *Angel by Giotto. Boville, S. Pietro Ispano.*

examples of mosaic work are both numerous and interesting.

A dominating theme of Sicilian mosaic work is the gold background. Golden decoration was used in Rome with considerable sobriety and served merely to highlight or underline details. But in Sicily the golden surface extends right across the work and becomes a major part of the composition. This particular style, which seeks to create an atmosphere of enchantment, is obviously strongly influenced by the East and suits the temperament of two widely opposed regions of Italy. Lavagnino writes[64] that for barely sixty years, between 1140 and 1200, there was an enormous output of mosaics and, by a strange historical phenomenon the two great centres in which this eastern style flourished in the twelfth century were Sicily and Venice.

It is well known that the commercial contacts between Sicily, Greece and Asia Minor were always strong and continued with full energy during the period of the Norman kings. At the same time in Venice there was a great period of artistic endeavour, during which San Marco was built which so clearly reflects the luxurious spirit of the East. Mosaic was the natural complement to this taste in architecture and so it is that those evangelical and biblical illustrations which we admire so much today were constructed at Palermo, Cefalu and Monreale, as at Venice. There are various opinions as to the identity of the artists that worked in Sicily. Lavagnino[65] suggests that the Norman kings made a point of bringing into their country 'oriental luxury and sought out artists who were trained in the great pictorial tradition of Byzantium', for they felt themselves to be the inheritors of the Arab court. Unfortunately many works have been lost, but a large number still remain intact. Indeed the quantity of the work is startling when one considers that in the cathedral at Monreale (Plate 43) alone one can admire more than six thousand square metres of figured mosaics. Contemporary with these are the works in the cathedral at Cefalu (Plate 42), undertaken in 1148, and those of the church of Santa Maria del'Ammiraglio, also known as the 'Martorana' (Plate 41), which show the portraits of Ruggero II (Plate 44) and of the Patriarch George of Antioch. The whole work is filled with an atmosphere of enchantment suggested by the gold background shimmering in the sunlight and barely reflects the cult of catholicism. The Palatine chapel has famous mosaics in the choir and transept which are considered to be of the same period as that at which the building was finished, that is during the reign of Ruggero II, between 1140 and 1150. The mosaics of the principal nave and those which remain in the lateral nave of the Palatine chapel may be dated to between 1150 and 1160. The cathedral at Monreale, however, is of a slightly later date and was probably decorated between 1174 and 1182. Among the earliest works – those in the Martorana and the cathedral of Cefalu and in the transept and choir of the Palatine chapel – can be found refined Byzantine forms, even though, according to Lavagnino, they are the work of several hands and betray various styles, sometimes clearly oriental and sometimes with Hellenistic touches.

But the refinement of the decorative taste recalls Greece as well as Byzantium. Lavagnino[66] writes: 'In the most ancient mosaics of the Palatine are to be seen rows of saints, mobile and lifeless in their vestments like marvellous chrysalises, with their eyes filled with holy thoughts and compassionate understanding. Yet next to them there are scenes

41 *Mosaic representing the Death of the Virgin. The background is gold and the tesserae multi-coloured. Palermo, church of 'La Martorana'.*

where everything is refined and set in the gradations of gold of the background, with a sense of distance and perspective according to the principles of classical tonal work.' The tesserae are almost always squared off, small, and so neatly placed in their rows as to make the joints almost invisible. They are of marble and vitreous pastes. The effect is certainly fascinating and anyone who enters the Martorana feels himself suddenly in a luminous golden box, surrounded by these beautiful figures that recall oriental and Greek mosaics. Lavagnino writes:[67] 'But in the mosaics of Monreale and also elsewhere in minor naves, although the construction may be less fine, there is progressively the feeling of a flight from Byzantine unreality and an inclination towards naturalistic forms. The composition of the scenes also is along strictly narrative lines and the grouping of the figures has been inspired by reality. For this reason I agree with the French critic who sees in these pieces the work of Italian craftsmen employing a Byzantine style. Is it not true that in the solemn architecture of the church we can feel some of the majestic moods of classical times?'

It does indeed seem that one should attribute this work to an Italian hand, whether for the numerous classical references, for the composition that differs so much from the Byzantine scheme, or for a sense of human movement and a greater plasticity. In these respects the pieces are notably different from those ancient works at Ravenna.

Sicilian mosaic decoration was employed by the Normans in their dwellings and palaces as well as in their churches. There are for example such decorations at Zisa (1190) and others in the so-called Room of King Ruggero in the tower of the 'Sacred Palace' at Palermo which imitate Byzantine work.

Diffusion and Decadence of Christian Mosaic Work

We now come to the church of St Sophia in Istanbul, which has become a mosque. The only sixth-century mosaic that has been preserved consists of a few fragments in the vestibule (Plate 45). While in Rome at this period churches were decorated with mosaic, in Byzantium the art was much more diffused.

Constantine transferred the seat of the Empire to Byzantium in 330 and under his dominion a law was passed which protected mosaicists from any taxation. His successors followed his example and a school of mosaicists was formed in the region of the Bosphorus, whose artists had at their disposal the finest models, even if they themselves did not reach such heights.[68]

While sculpture prevailed in the West, at Byzantium the major artistic medium was mosaic, and the churches, with their characteristic central plan, provided a definite place for every decorative figure in relation to the architectural structure. Important also is the influence of two iconoclastic periods[69] (726–787; 815–843) during which the pictures of the saints which decorated the apses were destroyed and replaced by a single cross on a gold background (Church of the Dormition at Nicaea; St Irene, Istanbul, and St Sophia, Salonika). In the church of the Blacherne, Constantine V replaced a cycle of Christological scenes with decorations of animals, plants and birds. From the ninth to the fourteenth century, the best period of Byzantine architecture, mosaics were much used.

Kitzinger[70] observes with good reason how three-dimensional effects were obtained in mosaics both by the inclination of tesserae and by the variety of coloured elements. It is interesting to follow the various Greek and

Byzantine influences which have left unmistakeable traces behind them. Greek work can be distinguished by the lines of the figures and the expressions of the faces, as well as by the folds and drapery of the gowns. Byzantine mosaicists gave themselves wholeheartedly to their work and achieved such fine effects by exploiting to the full the technical resources of their craft, so as to make the most of the effects of light upon the range of colours. They were especially successful between the sixth and tenth centuries. Among their greatest achievements was the use of gilded tesserae over the entire background, which made the figures seem to stand away in relief.

It is important to understand that from the time of the greatest development of mosaics in Byzantium, portable icons were built, some of which date from the period of the Paleologues, and consequently this type of mosaic is assumed to have begun during the eleventh century. These portable icons were rather thin tablets of wood, to which the tesserae were fixed either with gum mastic or with special adhesives made from wax.

It has already been shown how the fashion for black and white mosaic which was so widespread in the Roman era waned during the early Byzantine period and had almost disappeared from all the areas of the Mediterranean before the end of the reign of

42   *St Peter, St Vincent, St Lawrence, St Gregory, St Augustine and St Silvester. Cefalu, cathedral.*

43   *The story of Abraham and Esau. Monreale, cathedral.*

44 *Christ crowning King Ruggero II. Palermo, church of 'La Martorana'.*

Justinian.[71] Outside Italy during the Romanesque period tesserae mosaic was quite widely used in north-western Europe and according to Kitzinger[72] it was used in association with *opus sectile* which had been developed also in the medieval period of Byzantium. In Southern Italy, the end of the fifth century or the beginning of the sixth saw the mosaic work of the Baptistery of San Giovanni in Fonte at Naples which shows oriental influence, as may also be noted in San Prisco and Santa Maria Capua Vetere and in the Oratory of Casa Ramello near Otranto. While relatively few pavement mosaics were made during the Romanesque period, there were a number of interesting mosaics in Northern Europe and in many parts of Italy: in St Gereon in Cologne, at St Denis, in St Rémy at Reims and also at Osta, Turin, Vercelli, Novara, Casale Monferrato, in the church of San Michele at Pavia, and of San Savino at Piacenza; at Cremona in San Benedetto Po, at Ravenna in San Giovanni Evangelista, at Pesaro, at Brindisi, and in the most famous case in the cathedral of Otranto,[73] where in the twelfth century a splendid carpet of polychrome tesserae was made of a very hard local limestone (Plate 46). The themes are chosen from biblical subjects and the symbolic figures show the literary tendencies of Alexandrine, Carolingian and Breton mythological cycles. This pavement occupies the entire nave and depicts a great tree with many branches, among which are symbolic animals and human figures, highly shaded and in lively colours. The piece continues in the presbytery, the apse and the lateral nave, where whole pages of theology are illustrated by means of symbolic figures. It is one of the most important works to have come down to us in good condition from this period. The twelfth century in general has perhaps not been sufficiently appreciated, but its mosaicists laid the way which was to be taken by the artists of the Renaissance. A hundred years before Nicola Pisano and long before Cimabue and Giotto, mosaicists were making figures which were better designed and composed than those of the first Tuscan masters.[74] But during the thirteenth century the Tuscans above all lacked the decorative sense of the previous century and could not even equal the mosaicists who worked in Rome in the same period. Kitzinger attempts to find some explanation for this decadence in Tuscan mosaics; he suggests that it may have been caused by the arrival of Greek artists in the area, whose influence might have had a retarding effect upon the stylistic progress that had been made. Artistic achievement, however, did not disappear entirely. A typical representative of the movement of renewal which followed Masaccio was the well-known painter Alessio Baldovinetti (1425–1499). He studied the technical basis of the craft of mosaics which had been practically abandoned, and wrote a book on the subject and on the technique of stucco work. He himself, however, worked as a restorer of famous monuments and produced no original work. He restored, among other things, the dome of the Baptistery of San Giovanni and the ancient mosaics of San Miniato al Monte, both in Florence.

During the fourteenth century the Venetian schools were producing rather lifeless work of dubious taste, and in this they were followed by the mosaicists of the Vatican, who limited their output to producing copies of famous pictures. The fifteenth century saw few great works produced in Italy, apart from those already mentioned, and the craft was generally taken up by artists whose main preoccupation was painting. In fact the attention

45 *Anonymous Byzantine mosaic representing Christ. Istanbul, St Sophia.*

of Tuscany and other areas was turned rather in the direction of crafts which required more minute work, such as gold and silver work and jewellery. Indeed mosaics themselves betray unusual attention paid to elegant detail which tends to dispel the freshness which was a quality of earlier work.

Towards the end of the sixteenth century the Reverenda Febbrica Pontificia del Mosaico – or 'Reverend Pontifical Workshop for Mosaics'[75] – was established in Rome under the direction of Muziano Gerolamo of Brescia (1528–1592), and the patronage of Pope Gregory XIII. The workshop was at first located near the Gregorian Chapel, then moved to the ground floor of the Palace of the Archpriest and Cardinal of St Peter's behind the present Sacristy, and finally to the courtyard of San Damaso, where it flourished particularly during the papacy of Benedict XIII.

Another institution in Rome was the *Camera Apostolica*. This was directed by the Cardinal Bursar, and undertook the maintenance of monumental buildings. With the papacy of Urban VIII (1623–1644) there was much innovation in mosaic work, since this Pope had the idea of reproducing in mosaics ancient paintings in the Vatican. It is not hard to imagine the result of this scheme. Although it was by no means an original idea – examples of such copying have survived from ancient Rome – it was one which more thoroughly established mosaics on the road of decadence. All freshness was lost and replaced by the stale dullness of the copyist; furthermore the enlarging or cutting down of works – which were in any case often quite distorted in reproduction – in order to fit them into some specific space, led to results which often bordered upon the absurd. Nonetheless these works were produced in quantity, and many of them are still extant. The decorations of St Peter's are numerous and, apart from the pieces just discussed, mention must be made of the work of such artists as Pietro Berrettini da Cortona (1595–1669) who produced the cartoons for the Chapel of St Sebastian – another mosaicist, Guido Ubaldo Albatini (1600–1656), also worked at these – and those for the Chapel of SS. Sacramento. The lantern of Michelangelo's cupola is decorated with mosaics, as were the dome and the brackets. This work was begun during the papacy of Clement VIII (1592–1605). It is certainly not a great work of art, but it does merit a mention, if only because this century was otherwise so exclusively devoted to painting, sculpture and fresco. Gerspach observes how few critics treat the mosaics of the period together with other media, as they clearly should be: mention of them is almost entirely restricted to monographs on individual subjects. It is the very materials of mosaics that permit the achievement of effects peculiar to the craft, even when the artist is limited to some traditional pictorial subject. Thus even the mosaics of the cupola of St Peter's offer results that it would be difficult to obtain with a brush. The figures of the popes and bishops in the first circle, of the Redeemer, Virgin and apostles in the second, and of the angels with the instruments of the Passion in the third, are all of startling dimensions. Apart from the didactic aspect of the works, mention must be made of the problems of judgement involved in composing them so that they might be viewed clearly at great distance. The artists involved were Giuseppe Cesari or Giuseppino, also known as Cavalier d'Arpino (1568–1640), who produced the cartoons of the cupola and Marcello Provenzale da Cento (1577–1639) who collaborated in the decoration of the Clementine

46 *Details of a twelfth-century pavement mosaic made of multi-coloured* tesserae *cut from a local calcareous stone. Otranto, cathedral.*

Chapel and the cupola, and was a pupil of Paolo Rossetti.

Of this very able mosaicist it is known that he undertook a great deal of restoration work, and that he was especially knowledgeable in ancient techniques. He was an initiator of the fashion for using the tiniset tesserae in order to produce the effects of painting. Muziano, who was highly regarded by Michelangelo, was an academician at San Luca, and was nominated superintendant of the works at the Vatican by the Pope. Another mosaicist, Giovan Francesco Romanelli (1610–1662), was a pupil of Pietro da Cortona and was invited to the French Court by Cardinal Mazarin, who charged him with the work in the Louvre and in his palace. These are mannered mosaics in which all the figures look alike and the designs lack the vigour of those of earlier centuries. They are the work of large studios which were commissioned to execute predetermined designs; and, apart from the rare exceptions we have mentioned, the craftsmen were guided by masters who themselves lacked any special gifts. As during the earlier period of decadence, there was much making of small portable mosaics, designed to be seen from close up, which necessitated the use of tiny tesserae to produce shading which closely resembled oil painting. Even portraits were produced in this manner; but their value is limited and their interest purely historical. Apart from the St Peter's pieces there are few works of this period in Rome that warrant individual mention; among them is the mosaic at San Cesareo, after a design by Cavalier D'Arpino.

The development of a new kind of mosaic, which achieved its effects by exploiting the natural colours of hard stone, will be examined in detail in a later chapter. This was in fact the new direction in which mosaic was

47 *Detail of a pulpit in multi-coloured Cosmati mosaic. The main part of the mosaic is inlaid in a large panel of white marble. Capua, cathedral.*

able to develop, and which may still, moreover, produce fresh progress today. The history of mosaics proper may be continued by reference to the later façade of the cathedral at Florence, to the series of decorations on the façade of the cathedral at Orvieto and to other contemporary work. But although such symmetry and rather unimaginative cleanliness of design is often described disparagingly as 'picture postcard' work, it is pessimistic to assume that this ancient art is gone for ever. A sympathetic change of taste and of times could bring it back to life.

At the beginning of the nineteenth century an artist of the *Pontificia Fabbrica del Vaticano*, called Belloni, established himself in Paris and began to work on mosaics. His work was successful, and he received official recognition. A national studio was established for him in the Rue de l'Université, and young deaf-mutes who had been trained in the craft at the Ecole Impériale worked with him.

The school itself was placed under the direction of the Beaux-Arts, and the students were maintained there at government expense. Usually their work was simply copied from pictures, and consisted of *intarsio* work in the 'Florentine manner', generally miniatures. They may have been of *commesso* work, since this was a form of mosaic which was much prized at that time.

The most important products of this French studio which was founded by an Italian is in the Melpomene room at the Louvre. It is a large compartmented mosaic showing, in the centre, Minerva on a chariot escorted by Peace and Abundance. Symbolic representations of the Nile, Danube and Po are also figured, together with trophies of arms recording French victories. It is pervaded with neo-classical coldness, the design being by Baron Gérard and the colouration obtained by mixing marbles and enamels. Similar works were being produced in Florence, though they show greater coherence and employ natural hard stones. At the 1832 Exhibition much of Belloni's work was on show under the gradiose title of 'The Royal Manufacture of Mosaics of Paris, directed by Belloni and under the special protection of the King'. Among other pieces there figured a table of Corsican granite, bordered with olive leaves and a mosaic depicting doves. It is interesting to note that Belloni, presumably under influence from Florence, was also experimenting with granites. It would seem that shortly after the above date this institution produced no more work; certainly later pieces were of poor quality.

Subsequently, in 1876, a national school of mosaics was established in France and Gerspach, a member of the administration of the Beaux-Arts de France, was sent by the Minister to Rome to help develop the school. The French ambassador obtained permission from Pius IX to import into France artists from the *Fabbrica Pontificia*, and Poggesi, another Italian, was appointed head of the new school. Gerspach[76] wrote that 'Italy is the country of origin of mosaics', and he informs us that many Frenchmen learned the craft at the school he helped to establish.

The examination of all these works has shown the decline of mosaic art which began in the thirteenth century when pride of place went to painting, a medium through which perspective – and so the sense of volume and space – may so easily be rendered. Yet as Kitzinger[77] comments, mosaic work has its own special qualities, chromatic effects and a superior longevity, which should speak for its reputation. Although mosaicists strove to rival the popularity of painting they failed to do so, partly through the increasing taste for

work by 'masters', a taste which cannot be met by the craftsmanly skills of mosaic. The attempts of mosaicists to obtain the fine detail of painting by employing ever-smaller tesserae led them finally to reduce their elements almost to dust; the results were quite to the contrary of their aspirations, and indeed signalled the death of the art.

Cosmati Work

A type of mosaic which differs wholly from other kinds as far as technique is concerned is that known as 'Cosmatine'. Useful only in decorative work, it was first developed towards the end of the twelfth century. It was obviously inspired by Arabic pieces which had probably been seen in Sicily, and consists of highly-coloured geometric designs, the execution of which required a most unusual patience. The medium lent itself easily to the partial decoration of such objects as pyxes, doorposts, rose-windows, architraves and ledges, as well as entire pavements. It involved small triangular or square elements, which were repeated endlessly to form various patterns, usually star-shaped, and which were cut by hand from red porphyry, green serpentine, and white or other coloured marbles. The work thus involved the utilisation of hard stone.

The name of this type of mosaic work derives from that of an impressive dynasty of architects-decorators who produced buildings and decorated numerous churches and monasteries 'between 1170 and 1240. The founder of the dynasty must have been Lorenzo Tabaldo, father of Jacopo and grandfather of Cosma, who was in his turn father of Jacopo and Luca. What may well have been another branch of the family – a supposition which may be supported by stylistic similarities – is represented first by Cosma di Pietro Mellini, father of Jacopo, Giovanni, Deodato and Pietro. There is also a branch known as the Vassalletti, the eldest being Ranuccio, while others were Giovanni and Guittone, sons of Niccolo Pietro di Maria, and so on.'[78]

One of the most celebrated members of the family, Cosma, son of Jacopo, produced the portico of the cathedral of Civita Castellana in collaboration with his father. Other family activities, stretching across two centuries, include the enrichment of fine churches in Rome, the monasteries of San Paolo, San Lorenzo fuori le Mura, San Giovanni in Laterano; and also the construction of various minor churches in Lazio, the Marches, the Abruzzi, Umbria and Rome itself, which contain the finest of pavements, worthy of the term *opus tessulare*.

They made much use of gold leaf sandwiched in between vitreous elements which gives a particularly brilliant reflection. Important works of theirs still remain in Santa Maria Aracoeli and in Santa Maria in Cosmedin. Other pieces include the Portico of San Tommaso in Formis and that of the church of Sant' Antonio in Rome, the cloister of the Abbey of Sassovivo near Foligno; later is the pulpit of the cathedral at Capua (Plate 47) which is today in the crypt, the pulpit at Terracina, and the decorations at Sessa Aurunca, the pulpit in the cathedral at Salerno, various pieces at Cava dei Tirreni – and many other works, so filled with decorations, both sculptural and mosaic, as to make one think of that *horror vacui* of the pre-Roman period, although this is all refined work of good taste. Among important works undertaken elsewhere, special mention must be made of the pavement in the presbytery at Westminster Abbey, the work of Pietro and

Odesirio in the second half of the thirteenth century. As to dating in general, Jacopo I (to mention the most famous figures in the family) worked mainly between the end of the twelfth and the beginning of the thirteenth centuries; Cosma from 1210 to 1240; Luca and Jacopo II in the first half of the thirteenth century. Even then the fecundity of this creative family was not exhausted, however, since Cosma di Pietro Mellini had four sons who followed the family vocation between the thirteenth and fourteenth centuries.

II. INTARSIO WORK

Some explanation of the technical differences which characterise and identify intarsio work as opposed to mosaic must be given here. The essential distinction between the two, *intarsio* and mosaic work, as it is to be understood here, is that in the former the support is visible and constitutes the basis, whereas in the latter, which is nothing more than incrusted, the support has no importance and may be totally independent from the decorated surface, be it a pavement, a wall, a vault or a ceiling, or above all in portable compositions. *Intarsio* may be composed upon wood, ivory, metal or stone. No matter which of these is chosen, it is necessary first to engrave a design on to the surface, so that some polishable material may be inlaid into it, and so form the decoration. This engraved design is known as the *cassa* (Plate 48).

The *cassa* is then filled with a plug of different colour, whose shape corresponds exactly to that of the vertical section of the *cassa*, and generally fixed with gum mastic or some appropriate adhesive.

This book deals only with *intarsio* work in marbles or hard stones, since other media fall outside its scope. Some examination will be made both of such work in architecture and portable pieces, and there will be a brief description of the history of the art, the development of which corresponds rather closely to that of painting. As to etymology, *intarsio* is synonymous with *tarsia*; it may be translated approximately as 'inlay work', and comes from the Latin *tarsus* and the Greek *tarsos*,

48 *Example of a* cassa, *carved out in a slab of marble into a floral motif.*

49 *Pavement mosaic of* intarsio *work. Venice, S. Marco.*

meaning a trellis grating, or basket-work weave.

The prefix 'in', which in Latin means 'in a space either two or three dimensional', seems to enforce the intended meaning of *tarsio*, since various elements are placed in a 'grating' etched out from a surface with a scalpel or other apposite tool. In general the term applies to work such as gemsetting, damascening, marquetry and so on. The three 'pictorial' techniques we have mentioned – mosaics, *intarsio* and *commesso* work – are so similar that they are easily mistaken for one another, and often interchangeable. There are for example mosaics that have been inlaid into marble, and which in consequence are both 'mosaic' and '*intarsio*' at the same time. True *intarsio* however occurs when the base

50 *Panel of the cathedral at Capua showing Cosmati work.*

material into which the design is inlaid forms itself an essential element in the resulting decorative effect.

Intarsio always has a smooth or polished surface, and can achieve none of the effects of chiaroscuro and movement that mosaics can by means of the position of the tesserae. There is always a rather rigid, flat appearance in the work, however hard the artist may strive to avoid it.

Intarsio like mosaic has a long history. Michelangelo Cagiano di Azevedo[1] mentions that such work was produced in Egypt from the time of the First Dynasty onwards. It consisted largely of small pieces such as little caskets in wood and ivory. In Asia Minor during the same period (third millenium B.C.) *intarsio* has wide application, including work on architecture, the materials employed being hard stones and shells fixed by means of bitumen. The above-mentioned author includes the Standard of Ur in this category, but in my opinion this particular work is an example of mosaic. Vitreous pastes were much employed to give colouring and translucency, and small panels were made with these during the first half of the second millenium, a custom which was popular until the Ptolemaic period at the end of the second and the first centuries B.C.

The civilisation of Crete produced figurines inlaid with such various materials as rock crystal, wood, mother-of-pearl and precious metals. To the same culture belong vast decorations of alabaster on the façades and internal walls of palaces. In Roman times there is a reference to this type of work in Pliny.[2] He writes of *incrustatio* and *loricatio*, meaning respectively 'cover with a crust' and 'cover with a plating'. It is not entirely clear, however, whether the reference is to mosaics or to *intarsio*.

The crossover point from mosaic to *intarsio* is a gentle and natural one; even if a paving is not entirely covered with tesserae, its back-

51 *Twelfth-century* intarsio *work on the pavement of the Baptistery of S. Giovanni, Florence.*

ground mortar becomes less and less important visually as the number of tesserae increases. One thus arrives at such work as the *pavimentum scutulatum*, or lozenge (*scutulae*) paving[3] constructed in the Temple of Capito-

93

52 Intarsio *decoration on the base of Giotto's Campanile, Florence.*

53 *Portal with* intarsio *work. South side of Florence Cathedral.*

line Jupite after the Third Punic War. A similar trellis of lozenges is to be found at Athens situated in the orchestra area of the Theatre of Dionysus.[4]

An incrustation should always stand clear of its bed; it should merely bear upon it. As to origins, Pliny seems to attribute the introduction to Rome of *intarsio* as understood in the present study to Mamurra who was a Roman knight from Formia, and whose rank was *praefectus fabrorum*, in Caesar's army in Gaul. Certainly much polychrome *intarsio* is to be found during the period. Examples are to be found at Herculaneum in the House of the relief of Orestes and in later houses at Ostia.

As has previously been mentioned, some authors refer to *intarsio* as *opus interrasile* (mentioned by Pliny, *Historiae Naturalis*, xxxv), since this refers to a shallow plate introduced into a hollow formed in the main sheet.

Intarsio is normally purely decorative, and is rarely used for descriptive expression to which mosaic lends itself so naturally. Apart from Pliny's suggestion, it is hard to ascribe a close date for the appearance of *intarsio* in Rome, although this has not prevented numerous students from offering hypotheses about various times of its arrival.

The lack of clear distinction between *intarsio*, mosaic and other forms of inlay has led some authors to describe the decorations of the sarcophagus of Junius Bassus as inlay work. It appears rather, however, to be *opus sectile*, since the marble elements are simply laid upon a base and are not included within it.

Among noteworthy pieces are those in Orthodox Baptistery at Ravenna, where remarkable mosaic work is also to be seen. The *intarsio* work on the walls consists of finely inlaid foliate patterns and of geometric decorations with lozenges, rounds and rectangles.

Intarsio work is also common enough in the pavements of many paleo-Christian churches at Rome. Examples are to be found in: San Stefano Rotondo, the Lateran Baptistery, San Giorgio al Velabro, Santa Costanza, Sant' Agnese. The pavement of San Marco at Venice is in large part made of *intarsio* (Plate 49). The art of the Cosmati discussed earlier provides numerous examples of *intarsio* including work executed with triangular tesserae which are well suited to inclusion in marble surfaces and either decorate the architecture or occur over the entire surfaces of pavements (Plate 50).

The work on the great central paved floor of the church of San Miniato al Monte in Florence was begun in 1207 according to a date included in an inscription in the first frame. It is completely inlaid with *intarsio* of black and white marble, depicting the signs of the zodiac, animals and geometric patterns

54 *Pavement by D. Beccafumi showing large areas of* intarsio *and details scratched in which are reminiscent of the* niello *technique. Siena, cathedral.*

along the various borders, including rounds, star shapes, leaves, palms and lozenges. The overall design is pleasing and the work is so finely executed that it gives the impression of embroidery. In Florence also is the pavement of the baptistery of San Giovanni (Plate 51), together with the marble banding on the exterior of the same building and on the façade of Santa Maria Novella. In the latter, the outlines of the panels have been inlaid with rectangular strips of green marble, while small decorations have been introduced into the centres, above all in the large *tondi*, the lateral volutes, the almost triangular segments and the whole bottom part of the tympanum.

Gustave Soulier's[5] interesting work upon oriental influence in Tuscan painting contains references to pieces of *intarsio* work that have motifs comparable to oriental work. This author also notes that both Giotto and Arnolfo were inspired by the Cosmati to make use of *intarsio* in the complex of Santa Maria del Fiore (Plates 52, 53). Similar motifs reappear in Arnolfo's ciborium of San Paolo fuori le Mura, in Santa Cecilia in Trastevere, and in the tomb of Cardinal de Braye at Orvieto. Soulier writes:[6]

'Various periods are to be distinguished in the marble *intarsio* work in Tuscany. The first begins in Florence with the decoration of San Giovanni, and continues immediately with that of San Miniato al Monte. Within the same phase fall the works in the abbey at Fiesole and in the cathedral at Empoli. The second period during the twelfth century includes the exterior decorations of the cathedral at Pisa, and upon the cathedral and the church of San Michele at Lucca, together with various other work on church furniture during the twelfth and thirteenth centuries. A third period embraces work upon the pavements in the baptistery of San Giovanni at Florence and of San Miniato al Monte, as well as the decoration upon the façade of the latter (thirteenth century).

'These various periods all show oriental workmanship and mannerisms. Within a fourth period may be grouped fourteenth-century work, principally that on the lateral façade and on the transept of Santa Maria del Fiore and the Campanile. This type of work became truly well adapted to Florence and underwent various evolutionary changes until the original manner was lost. To a fifth period may be attributed the work of Leon Battista Alberti on the façade of Santa Maria Novella (1470), which displays even later influences. Here, however, only the three earliest phases displaying purely oriental influence need concern us.'

Soulier's work helps us to understand how this oriental influence came to bear upon *intarsio* work in Tuscany.

Interest in chromatic effects obtained by the inclusion of coloured marbles is to be noted in many late Romanesque buildings. Pulpits, baptismal fonts and screens with *intarsio* work are to be found in Campania, Lazio and southern Italy. In the paving of the cathedral at Siena *intarsio* work acquires a particular importance, since in this case the artists have used various methods of achieving figurative expressions and have had great success. These Siena masterpieces were achieved by the use of many different materials: in the sheets of white marble, furrows of a black pitch mixture have been inlaid in a manner that recalls inlaid enamel work on metal. The method lends itself to the representation of figures far better than marble itself would. The figures are often simply marked out on the background with furrows of limited depth in which drilled holes are

55 *Detail of floor by L. Maccari. Siena, cathedral.*

spaced. Pieces of marble would certainly not have been suitable inlay into these. The artists then joined up the various sections by means of the engraved furrows so that the figures give the appearance of wholeness.

This system was much employed by Domenico Beccafumi for his vigorous biblical scenes (Plate 54), but its greatest disadvantage is that it resists badly to the wear caused by the continual passage of feet. An entirely different system was used by Matteo di Giovanni for his grandiose design of the 'Slaughter of the Innocents' which lies close to the Nicola Pisano pulpit. In this the *intarsio* is realised by means of marbles that vary in colour from Sienese Yellow and Maremma Red to green and grey. These too have furrows filled with pitch paste, while they also

56 *Detail of floor by L. Mussini. Siena, cathedral.*

contain large monochrome areas where the shape of the marble alone gives the outline of the figures. This system resembles closely that of *commesso* work in hard stones, which will be discussed further on. The cathedral at Siena is also decorated with *intarsio* in the central nave, as well as in the minor naves and in the transept (Plates 55, 56) with various designs which are repeated in the Baptistery. Francesco di Giorgio Martini prepared the cartoons for the decorated paving to be found in the chapel of Santa Caterina in the church of San Domenico in the same city. It should also be noted that the great double windows of the cathedral at Florence have the frames ornamented (Plate 57) with the finest *intarsio*, and there is similar work everywhere on the marble surfaces of the great edifice, the design of which is most interesting even in the high areas which are not normally visible (Plate 58). Motifs vary from simple stylised flowers at the centre of panels to complicated designs at the crowns of the arches that consist alternately of geometric patterns in green and red marble circumscribed by circles and of corollas of flowers both positive and reversed, having borders of other white corollas on a green background. The results are most effective, and this is a particularly magnificent example of how *intarsio* work, together with sculpture, may be used to offset the monotony of white marble.

In the Giotto's Campanile the *intarsio* work is to be found largely in the upper areas of the building, beginning at the third floor and increasing in number as the building rises, until at the highest level they are to be seen in recurrent geometric patterns in the panels next to the great windows, in the triangles of the tympani and in the horizontal bands. It is reasonable to guess that in the lower part of the building executed by Giotto he preferred sculptural to flat decoration, and the latter certainly cannot achieve the effects of chiaroscuro obtainable with bas-relief and full-relief, and which may be observed in the photograph reproduced here (Plate 52).

Among the more singular uses of this type of decoration in southern Italy is that on the church of Santa Maria di Collemaggio in L'Aquila founded in 1287.[7] Here the same

57 *Polychrome marble* intarsio *work on the embrasure of the double windows of Florence Cathedral.*

58 *Exceptionally fine* intarsio *decoration representing a row of oil lamps above the so-called 'porta della Mandorla'. North side of Florence Cathedral.*

red and white motif is repeated over the entire rectangular façade in a simple and almost monotonous fashion. In the cathedral of Sessa Aurunca there is an abundance of the Cosmati type of mosaic which, especially in the fine pulpit with its ribbon-like motifs, combines influences both Arabic and Byzantine that recall similar work at Cava dei Tirreni, in the cathedral at Salerno, in Capua, Terracina, Calvi, Caserta Vecchia, San Giovanni in Toro, and in the cathedral of Ravello.[8]

At Rome in the Hall of Justice of the Castel Sant' Angelo, in Florence on the first floor of the Palazzo Vecchio, and above all in the Laurentian Library (Plate 59) are to be found fine inlays not made of marble but of terracotta. Among the finest is the brick pavement of the great salon on the first floor, described by Giorgio Vasari as the masterpiece of its kind. The panels are in various shades of red terracotta, which were obtained by various techniques of kilning, as well as different types of clay. The work is that of Santi Buglioni after a design by Tribolo,[9] and the piece is magnificent although fairly fragile. Within the meaning of the terms given earlier, the piece may be considered either as *intarsio* or as a sectional mosaic, since all its elements rest upon the floor. André Chastel[10] classifies it as the former.

Among the great baroque churches of Rome polychrome decorations abound. A fine example is the Capella Spada in San Gerolamo della Carità, which was based upon a design by Francesco Borromini who worked during the seventeenth century. The chapel was reconstructed after the church was rebuilt in 1660, and is conceived in the bizarre manner characteristic of the latter artist as a kind of room, the marble walls of which are decorated throughout with coloured floral intarsio.[11]

In Naples also, a triumph of inlay work can be seen in the grandiose church of the Charter-house of San Martino. Cosimo Fanzago of Bergamo worked on it in 1623 after Giovan Battista Dosio, and designed the greater part of the interior decoration. This is a rather special type of inlay which, in the paving, is really more *commesso* work, relying for its chromatic effects upon the characteristic veining of various marbles. It is executed in soft stones, however, that is in marbles of striking colour; these are used to great visual effect, and confront the spectator with a richly varied carpet of stone. Although many authors consider it to be *tarsio* work, it

59 *Magnificent pavement with* intarsio *work in terracotta by Santi Buglioni after a design by Tribolo. Florence, Laurentian Library.*

would certainly seem more correct to describe it as *commesso*. The pieces are cut in a summary manner, and the gaps between one element and the next are often quite irregular, in accordance with the prevailing taste of the period. The elements themselves are cemented directly into the foundation of the paving and cover the whole surface, giving it the desired impressive effect.

True *intarsio* work is to be found in the same church in the principal altar, the lateral altars of the numerous chapels, and in the curious baluster which surrounds the presbytery; in the latter hard and semi-precious stones have also been used. The seventeenth century in general, however, witnessed the decline of the use of marble *intarsio* and other inlays in mural and paving work, and its growing popularity instead as a decoration for furniture. Such furniture might be inlaid with wood, or have panels of semi-precious or hard stone inlay attached to it.

Vignola[12] occupied himself towards the middle of the sixteenth century with the production of inlaid and *intarsio* tables of various coloured marbles, and it was during this period that the taste for portable pieces began which was to undergo such amazing development. It was in Italy, and especially in Florence, that this art took root.

Some mention must be made of the history of the art in Asia and in the Orient in general. Periods of successful work were sometimes followed by periods of export – depending of course upon the political circumstances and fortunes of the countries concerned; the latter, unpleasant though they can be, never fail to make their mark upon the arts.

In the East, the magnificence of the architecture was a symbol of the power of the ruling classes and commanded the respect of the people, the brilliant colours of semi-precious stones were valued for this purpose, starting from the Indo-Islamic period.

The imperial residence of the Moghul ruler, Shah Jahan, who reigned from 1627 to 1658 at Delhi, was built of white marble – a material used in warm climates also for its functional properties – and contains interesting *intarsio* work which, just as in previous such residences, was made with soft, calcereous stones of various colours. H. Goetz[13] considers that the work is related to Florentine mosaics, and that the Florentine influence was carried thither by French and Italian soldiers of fortune. It is certain that in the case of the Taj-Mahal[14] there was a Florentine influence at work, both as to the manner in which the work is realised and as to the abundance of strongly coloured elements, among which are jaspers, agates, chalcedonies, cornelians, jades and turquoises. The design is not Tuscan, nor even European, however, but has a typically oriental character which shows especially in the angular curves of the leaves, the unusual outlines of the panels, and in the strange flowers which are certainly foreign to Europe.

There are very many areas of *intarsio* in the edifice, developed in infinite varieties of decorative form. There is a profusion of flowers, columns, verses from the Koran inscribed in Indian characters at the bases of cupolas and underlined by elegantly woven patterns. This represents a remarkable achievement which will be discussed in greater detail in the last chapter.

The disappearance or at least the decline of *intarsio* in India was signalled by this Moghul Emperor's tomb, in the first decade of the eighteenth century. Such work was replaced by painting on marble and also on stucco imitating marble which represented a clear step in the direction of the baroque.

103

This decline in popularity of both mosaic and *intarsio* work will provide the opportunity to evaluate the new art of 'Florentine *commesso* in hard stone', which saw such widespread development after the sixteenth century. This was to derive much of its character from mosaic work since it is also a pictorial art which inherits from the latter both its formal and essential characteristics. It also acquires the characteristics of *intarsio* when used decoratively in architecture; but it has qualities of its own which it owes to the siliceous nature of its materials, and which cannot be achieved by the use of soft, calcareous stones.

III. HARD STONES

What hard stones are and why they are so called is not easy to explain, especially since the word 'stone' itself is a vague term which may be applied to a vast gamut of compact, inorganic, non-saline materials, which have no connection with the stones usually employed as building materials. It therefore seems worthwhile to make a rapid digression which may clarify the concept of hard stones and which may be of assistance in understanding the historical and artistic assessment which follows. Such digression may also help the student to distinguish the numerous substitute materials which are used and which have aesthetic properties similar to those of genuine stones. Such substitute materials may be coloured to give the appearance of genuine materials; in other cases real stones of small value are treated chemically to give them the colouring of rarer and hence more valuable stones. Some imitation materials are so well counterfeited, even as to internal striations which result from stratification or compression, as to require close analysis in order to recognise them for what they are. Such materials are always distinguishable by the expert, however, and their value is correspondingly less than that of the genuine article.

To learn how the materials may be identified and classified by logical if not entirely scientific criteria, it is necessary to turn back to the end of the eighteenth and the early years of the nineteenth century when the German mineralogist Friedrich Mohs (1773–1839) studied and made public an important classification of minerals that was in opposition to the existing systems of Jacob Berzelius and Abraham Werner. He thus gave his name to his practical method for the determination of hardness of minerals which he proposed in 1822.

The standard he proposed was the ability of a given material to withstand scratching, and by this means minerals were arranged in a series ranging from the softest to the hardest. A previous system classified them as soft if scratched by a fingernail, semi-hard if scratched by steel, and hard if not scratched by steel. This unsatisfactory method was liable to gross error through the variable qualities of its standard models. Mohs' observations led him to base his system upon the following dictum: 'Of two minerals, the harder is the one that scratches the other'. He established a series of ten degrees of hardness by these means; but even these, useful though they are, have proved on rigorous analysis to have the defect that the intervals between them are not identical, and can therefore themselves lead to error. Modern techniques include the use of such apparatus as the sclerometer which permits the precise measurement of hardness. Such methods are not invariably applicable, however, since they necessitate penetration of the material which in the case of precious stones or works of art is clearly undesirable.

The generally accepted scale of hardness with its chemical references for each element is as follows: 1. Talc (acid semisilicate of magnesium); 2. Gypsum (hydrated sulphate of calcium); 3. Calcite (calcium carbonate); 4. Fluorite (calcium fluorite); 5. Apatite (fluorine phosphate or calcium chlorophosphate); 6. Feldspar (aluminium, potassium and sodium tricilicate); 7. Quartz (anhydrons oxide of silicon); 8. Topaz (fluoriferons orthosilicate of aluminium); 9. Corundum (sesquioxide of aluminium); 10. Diamond (pure crystallised carbon). It should be noted that many crystals have some variation of hardness between different facets, and indeed directional variations within the same facet; such complications have led scientists to establish a separate category of anisotropes. These variations must, of course, be taken into consideration by cutters of precious and ornamental stones, since they must try to ensure that the exterior faces of such stones will not be subject to wear.

The scale of minerals established by Mohs has been divided into three parts. Those that belong to the talc and chalk categories are known as 'soft'; the calcitic, fluoritic and apatitic categories are known as 'semi-hard'; while feldspar, quartz, topaz, corundum and diamond fall into the category of 'hard stones'. It would be interesting to make a collection of these ten stones; moreover it is not an expensive hobby, since splinters even of diamonds have no great value. From this explanation it will in any case be clear that 'hard stones' are those which fall in the categories between the sixth and tenth degrees of Mohs' Scale.

The word 'stone' is a very general one. It is as well to understand that further distinction is made between minerals and rocks. Minerals are those natural inorganic bodies which have a specific chemical composition showing constant characteristics. An interesting example of a mineral is provided by quartz, also known as rock crystal. Rocks on the other hand are those aggregates of various minerals which, in large independent masses, form the so-called earth's crust. These are divided into volcanic, sedimentary and metamorphic rocks. When such rocks are composed practically of single species of minerals, they are known as 'simple' – e.g. white marble is simple. Far more commonly, however, rocks are composed of two or more minerals, often distinguishable to the naked eye; thus granite is formed largely from quartz, feldspar and mica.

The distinction between calcareous and siliceous stones should also be understood. Calcareous stones are of medium hardness and are susceptible to attack by hydrochloric acid, whereas siliceous stones are hard and not susceptible to attack by hydrochloric acid.

It is worth repeating that this scientific parenthesis, while it has no direct connection with the history of art, is essential elementary knowledge for anyone who wishes to examine a work in hard stone, so that some idea is gained of how nature produces these mysteriously indelible colours and what chemico-physical characteristics distinguish them. The following brief account of the minerals and rocks used in *commesso* work must be limited for lack of space to the following large families: quartzes, chalcedonies, agates, jaspers, granites and porphyries (Plates 60, 61, 62), since these include most of the materials employed in *commesso* work. A few semi-hard materials are used and will be mentioned separately.

Quartz, when it is colourless and very transparent, is a mineral of 7 degrees of hardness. Frequently enough, however, it has colour of one kind or another, and such varieties have different names, such as the type of quartz called 'rock crystal'; when white and opaque it is known as 'milky quartz'. 'Smoky quartz' has a brown colour. Yellow quartz passes under the misleading name of 'topaz' (the latter is in fact an orthosilicate of aluminium). 'Amethystine quartz' or 'amethyst' has a very unstable and variable violet colour, and is used as a gem, although it, too, is quite different from the true amethyst that comes from the East, which is a variety of corundum.

We now come to the family of chalcedonies. These take their name from the city of Chalcedon in Bithynia (an ancient country of Asia Minor which lay between the Sea of Marmora, the Propontis, the Black Sea, Phrygia and Paphlagonia). They are a microcrystalline variety of quartz, having a very compact and rayed fibrous structure. Common chalcedony, which has a hardness of 6·5–7 degrees, shows no colour in thin sections if it is pure and translucent; but if it contains impurities it can assume different colours and may be banded in gently shaded gradations – a quality much exploited by makers of *commesso* work, and which has given rise to a nomenclature that refers to different tones and provenances. Cornelians are part of this family, and have a lively red colour, while the highly prized agate which is banded in concentric rings is another variety – the colour range of this stone is practically infinite.

Chrysoprase has a greenish or blueish colour due to a trace of nickel and may in thick pieces have a special transparency. Onyxes (perhaps from the coptic *uoein*, to shine, or from the Greek *onyx*, fingernail) are varieties with banded colours such as white and black, or white and red, the divisions between the colours being in gently shaded gradations as a result of diffusion of the colouring agents. Some varieties of quartz which have intrusions of asbestos and of ferric oxides change their colour according to the incidence of the light, and these occur in strange forms which have been given names that refer to their aesthetic rather than to their scientific qualities; e.g. 'falcon's eye', 'cat's eye', 'tiger's eye'.

Jasper is another variety of quartz; it is microcrystalline, compact and opaque. For these reasons it is used only for its reflective qualities and may have various speckled tints, banded or striated colours. Many jaspers in fact are mixtures of minerals and may therefore be classified as rocks. Opal – so much used as an ornamental stone – is a bioxide of hydrated silicon; it is milky as a rule but exists in many other variations such as the so-called 'fire opal' which shows very brilliant red lights.

Apart from hard stones, other minerals are sometimes used where their medium hardness and unusual colouring may be employed to advantage. One of these is lapis lazuli – a name that derives from both a Latin and an

60 1 *Dark Alsatian jasper;* 2 *Volterra jasper;* 3 *Orbicular Corsican granite;* 4 *Oriental chalcedony;* 5 *Bohemian jasper. Florence, Museo dell' Opificio.*

Arabic word, and means 'azure stone'. This is a complex silicate of aluminium and sodium with a hardness of about 5 degrees and a colour that varies from a light to an intense blue according to the provenance of the stones. Tiny particles of pyrites sometimes lend golden flecks to the material while other mineral intrusions such as calcites and micas give whitish and shiny effects. When polished it may have a brilliant and almost translucent appearance. It is found in Europe but more commonly in Afghanistan, Russia, Persia, China and the Andes.

Malachite is also much employed in *commesso* work. It has a green striated appearance, and is a carbonate of copper. Although of pleasing appearance it has a hardness of only about 4 degrees, and hence breaks easily, polishes poorly, and becomes opaque with wear. It is found in the Urals, Africa, Chile and Arizona.

So far as rocks are concerned mention must first be made of the vast family of granites, which are metamorphic in character and which are made up of quartz, orthoclase and mica. Their colour mainly derives from the orthoclase and may be white, pink or bright red. The name derives from the granular structure which may at times be polymorphic. Granite is principally to be found in the Scandinavian peninsula, South Africa and Corsica; but alkaline-calcitic granites are to be found almost everywhere. Hardness is between 6 and 7 degrees.

Porphyries are volcanic rocks, may be quartziferous or non-quartziferous, and show colours varying from a reddish tint to a muddy green. The Latin name *porphyrites* means crimson stone. Abundant in various areas of Germany, the most prized kinds are those known as 'paleo-volcanic porphyrites'.

Of great character are the antique Egyptian reds and the spotted antique greens that were much prized as building materials in ancient Rome and which are now very rare. Porphyries in general are very difficult to work, but have nonetheless been most popular in expensive statuary because of their colours and their polishing qualities. They are extremely hard, falling in the Mohs scale between 6 and 7 degrees, and in ancient times there was continual competition to find some trick by which they might easily be cut or ground away. Such secret formulae usually involved some tempering of the saw blade as soon as it was taken from the furnace by immersing it in the strangest of liquids, which it was hoped would impart their magical qualities to the blade, and which might contain a ram's head or some mixture of herbs. Science has given us surer means of producing particularly hard steels nowadays, but working porphyry is still laborious, and artists can produce fine work only at the expense of a great deal of time and energy.

Among hard stones a prominent position must be given to petrified woods, both for the nobility of their appearance and for their hardness. The process of petrification takes place over millenia when, in certain conditions, the woody fibres of the trees are replaced by silicates so that the internal and external appearance and colour of the wood is unchanged, but the structure acquires a hardness of 7 degrees. The material may be sliced into sections and polished to the same standard as jasper or agate. Whole forests of petrified trees have been found in Egypt, Germany, New Mexico, Arizona, France, and Madagascar.

Here are some notes upon the cutting and working of hard stones – a craft that has

remained almost unaltered through the ages since only purely manual methods produce satisfactory art works. There seems no doubt that machines produce lifeless work that cannot compare with that resulting from direct human intervention and skill. To cut and shape the materials, all that is required is a simple blade or wire oscillating horizontally (Plate 63). Such a blade or wire is whetted with emery – a crystalline substance generally made artificially from the combination of carbons with silicates – and it is this abrasive powder, having a hardness close to that of diamonds (9·5–9·7), which actually cuts through the material. The whetting process takes place upon a dampened blade, in which the emery or carborundum encrusts itself. Such incrustation takes place more successfully in a soft metal rather than in a hard one.

Much the same effect is obtained by glueing glass fragments to a card to produce the so-called glass-paper: an abrasive that is capable of cutting through metal.

When cutting with a blade or a wire it is possible to obtain sections of rock or mineral pieces that are one millimetre thick – or even less, according to the compactness of the material – and so produce fine effects of colour and translucency. It is by the arrangements of pieces cut from such sections that figures and patterns are obtained. To produce each element of the design from the sections, a system similar to that of fretwork is employed, but whereas in the latter case an iron wire blade is held in a steel bow, for hard stone a bow of chestnut wood is sufficient, which also holds a narrow iron wire (Plate 65). A hole is first bored into the section of stone to be cut (Plate 66); then the wire is introduced into it, whetted with water and emery, and tightened into its bow so that the desired cuts can be made. It is a slow process, however, for the material is hard. For practical reasons the angle of the cut must be inclined and not at right angles to the exterior plane of the piece, so that by subsequent adjustment with a simple steel file, a perfect join with the next piece may be obtained.

Even the first cuts from the raw materials must be made with care, since the interior colour of the materials may not correspond to the exterior, and many cuts may be necessary before the desired colour is matched. Occasionally faults may appear in the interior of the piece which render all the labour to no avail. Where the pebble is rounded, it probably has an internal stratification rather like that of an onion. Clearly if the cut is made longitudinally it will produce a section with a striped surface; if cut horizontally it will produce a section which reveals concentric circles.

Every stone has its own characteristics, and cutting into sections reveals differences that may vary infinitely both as to pattern and colour. Stones may be lined, banded, rayed or marbled, and may occur in the strangest shading and chromatic tone. It is clear that, given the gamut of such material, a table of variation might be prepared that would cover an immense range of appearances. The student of stones must possess at least an elementary knowledge of mineralogy and geology, and must know where to seek out those extravagantly tinted rocks which may assist the artist in his work. The discovery of these hidden colours has brought the mosaicist and the maker of *intarsio* into a new field which might be described as that of the miniature, since the word describes precisely the kind of work that the discovery of these qualities of stone led to. For such work the craftsman must have at his disposal as vast a range of material as possible, so that he can find the piece which interests him, and allows him most closely to achieve the effect he desires to make.

Tesserae mosaics do not permit such effects: they rely on being looked at from a distance; in this case detail is partly lost – it is the whole which is delightful. With hard stone there is no such limitation: the finest detail is obtainable if it is sought carefully enough.

61 *Overleaf left: 6 light Alsatian jasper; 7 Red porphyry; 8 Striped Arno jasper; 9 Petrified wood; 10 Persian lapis lazuli. Florence, Museo dell' Opificio.*

62 *Overleaf right: 11 German agate; 12 Oriental agate; 13 a rare example of agate showing a crystallization of amethyst quartz and a pale-blue central core; 14 agate jasper. Florence, Museo dell' Opificio.*

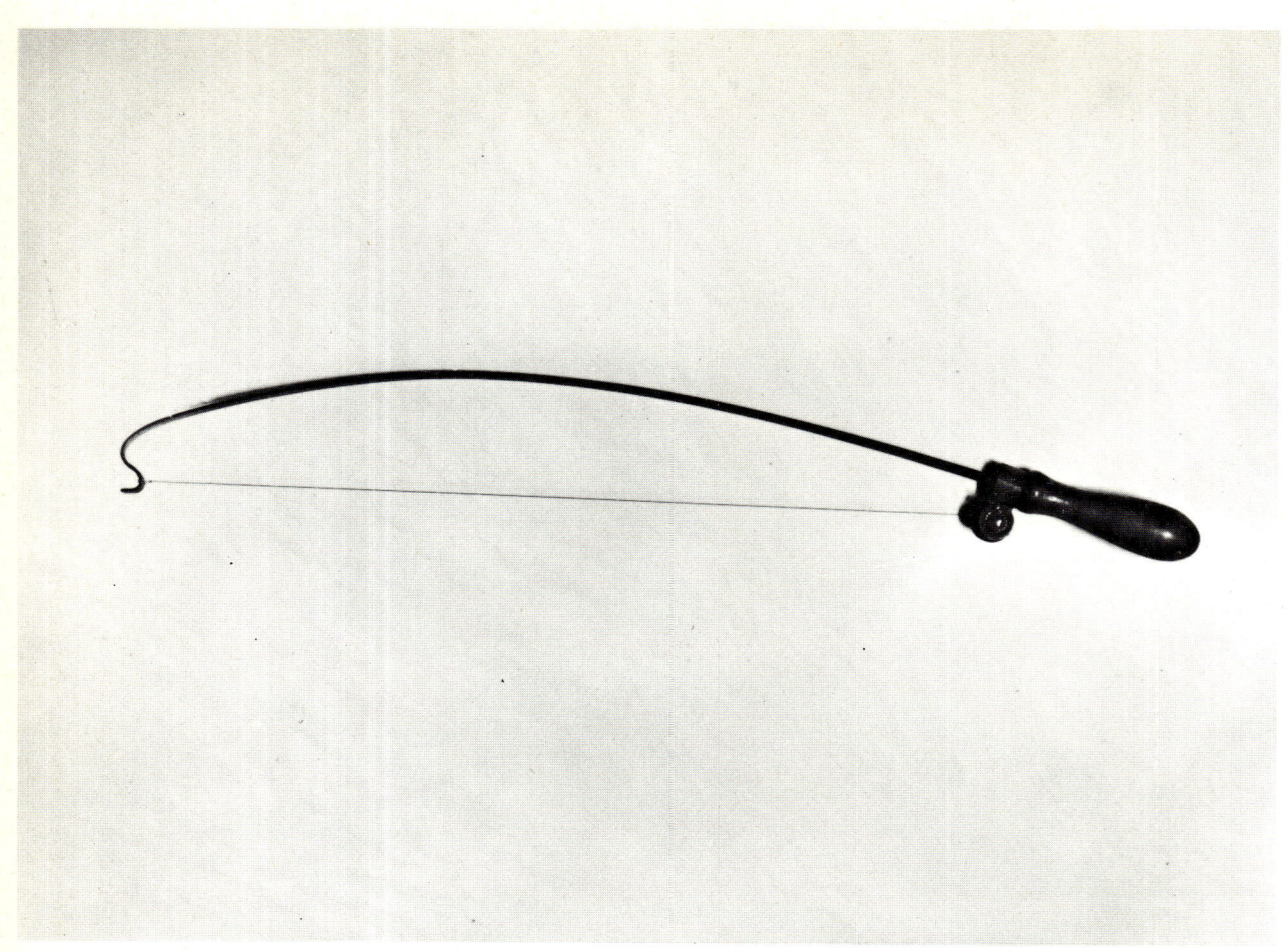

63   *Nineteenth-century hand-operated bow used to tighten the wire. Florence, Museo dell' Opificio.*

64   *Nineteenth-century bench used by* commesso *workers and gem cutters.*

65   *A mosaicist's bench showing the vice and bow file.*

66   *Nineteenth-century hand-operated drill used to make holes into the pieces which are to be cut. Florence, Museo dell' Opificio.*

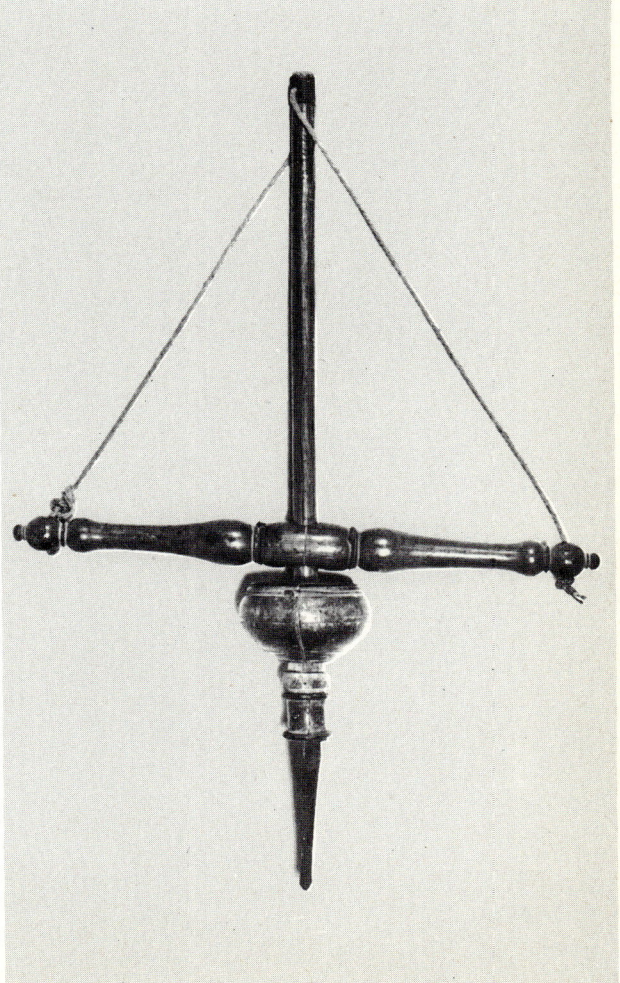

IV. COMMESSO WORK

The word *commesso* is the past participle of the verb *commettere*, and is derived from the Latin *commissus* meaning 'put together', 'joined'. The word was perhaps used for the first time in sixteenth-century Florence to describe those particular works of art in hard stone which are composed from large numbers of small pieces, placed tightly together and attached to some support with gum mastic or some other adhesive, to reproduce some pattern or design. The surface of this work may then be polished to a mirror smoothness, whereupon the single elements are lost in the effect of the whole.

Such work is usually known as 'Florentine Mosaic',[1] but although it has its roots in the type of mosaic work known as *opus sectile* which has been described earlier, it has many special features of its own which result from the emphasis upon choice of natural colours. It is really a kind of miniature art brought to a fine point of figural reality. Detail is reproduced with great precision by exploiting the natural markings of hard stones, which offer variations in appearance far more subtle and diverse than those to be found in calcareous or other soft stones.

It is fascinating to discover, in the heart of outwardly amorphous pieces of stone, patterns and shapes which bear an odd resemblance to the corollae of flowers, the tendrils of the vine, or the leaves of trees – a resemblance so close that it would be difficult to imitate it with a brush and paints. Again, it is possible to obtain effects which change according to the incidence of the light, rather as do the wings of certain butterflies and exotic birds. Such effects result from the presence of tiny micaceous elements in such minerals as labradorite and some kinds of quartz.[2]

This art has made it possible for the dreams of earlier mosaicists to come true, and the durability of the work is for all practical purposes infinite: neither time nor light can fade or alter. Zobi[3] quotes the following remarks of Baldinucci[4] concerning *commesso*: 'Be it known, therefore, that from the commencement of this noble art such superb works were and are still being made in the Gallery of the Serene Grand Duke, both in low and full relief, and far more often upon a single plane that, not merely do they compare with the finest painting of an object, but seem to be the very thing itself. Whereas a painter must be knowledgeable in the art of mixing and spreading the colours – already difficult to work with because of their very thinness – and blending them together with much skill so as to achieve, according to his needs, a whole range of half-tones which are completely different from the original colour; it is not so in *commesso* work where the crafts-

67 Commesso *work in soft stones representing the arms of the combined houses of Medici and Lorraine. It is made of Carrara marble, lapis lazuli, green porphyry, Spanish marble, Siena marble, red porphyry. Florence, Museo dell' Opificio.*

man – just as the painter – has to reproduce his subject-matter realistically, but not with materials the colours of which he can control and blend together. He must take into consideration the colour of his stone as nature formed it. Furthermore he has no opportunity to mix one colour with another to produce a third; rather he must discover precisely what he needs already formed in nature. But how does the artist reproduce gradations of tone, that may change unnoticeably from the lightest to the darkest in any colour? For this, it is necessary for him to seek and discover every shade that may be seen in the infinite diversity of colours which occur in nature; it is impossible unless he observes the great variety of markings that occur in hard gems and other stones. And so it is that he must be so practised in the observation of pictorial colour that he can recognise precisely what will serve him best, both internally and externally when he looks at a gem, to represent the thing he has in mind in all its tones. It is also part of his craft that his imagination must always be alive to the possibilities presented by his materials. There is no question of repeating work already done but for each occasion he must seek out precisely the stone he wants from a mountain of them, and then know how to place it to best advantage so that it precisely suits his particular needs.'

In order to acquaint the student with the origins and early development of the art of *commesso*, it is necessary to make some reference to the history of Florence during the three centuries when the Medici family was closely associated with it.[5] It is a curious fact that historians invariably particularly mention the precious vases, the jewellery and the hard stone work when writing of the period, almost as though they formed an integral part of the existence of this family.

The Medicis traded with the East; their banking activities stretched across what was then known of the entire world; they maintained close ties with the Papacy and hence with the Roman Court; family ties kept them in touch with France, Austria, Spain and Germany; and diplomatic relations were maintained with every monarch. Magnificent wedding presents and the gifts of visiting dignitaries contributed much to their fabulous treasury. But far more important was their own habit of acquiring antique objects, and they displayed a refined taste in their choice of gems and hard stones from the earliest Renaissance period, when possession of Greek and Roman objects was still rather unusual.

They bought oriental and antique Roman vases and had them mounted in gold and silver. Onyx, jasper, agate and rock crystal, finely worked and shining with inalterable splendour, fascinated those who had the opportunity to see them. Apart from collecting such ornaments, they decided to have some made for themselves, and if no artist was available in Florence to do the work required, then such men were brought from abroad, often from great distances.

In the mesh of history woven with wars, intrigues, splendours, griefs, victories and defeats, it is interesting to trace this particular family activity which was passed down like an inheritance and which time and again survived family catastrophe (Plate 67).

Zobi[6] informs us that the earliest Florentine inlayer of hard stones was Benedetto Peruzzi, who was mentioned by Scipione Ammirato in *Istorie fiorentine*, volume XIV, and who was living in Padua in 1379. But the workshops of the Florentine goldsmiths are known to have produced such considerable figures as Ghiberti, Brunelleschi, Donatello,

68 *Coat-of-arms of the City of Siena, made of jaspers, chalcedony and mother-of-pearl. Florence, Medici Chapels.*

Verrocchio, Pollaiuolo and Iacopo della Quercia.

After Peruzzi, Zobi next mentions Giovanni delle Corniole, son of Lorenzo di Pietro delle Opere. The latter was probably from Pisa, and painted the famous portrait of Savonarola in the time of Lorenzo the Magnificent, which is still to be seen in the gem collection of Florence in the Palazzo Pitti, and of which Vasari speaks ecstatically. Morassi[7] also mentions Pier Maria Serbaldi da Pescia as well as such masters as Antonio Pisano, Volterrano, and Neri Razzanti.

Lorenzo the Magnificent commissioned many craftsmen to cut cameos, make jewellery and work in hard stones, and it is known that at the Medici Court there worked Valerio Vicentino (mentioned by Vasari), Domenico Compagni (nicknamed 'dé camei', a Milanese who worked much in Florence and produced a togaed bust of Lorenzo in onyx), Matteo del Nassaro and Giovanni da Castel Bolognese.

Zobi[8] reports that at the time when he wrote there were: 'eighteen precious vases bearing the mark *Laur.Med.*. Of these, five are of oriental red onyx, four of red Sicilian jasper, two of amethyst, one of yellow Sicilian jasper, one of red Cypriot jasper, one of cornelian breccia, one of red amethystine jasper, another of flowered Sicilian jasper, one of Grisons jasper, and one of petrified wood. They were believed to be of medieval Egyptian workmanship, whereas today it has almost been proved that they are in some cases Byzantine and in others Venetian.'[9]

All these were gifts from Lorenzo's nephew, Pope Clement VII, to the Basilica Laurenziana in 1553; some were placed in the Medici residence of San Marco at Florence.

A splendid seal of Pope Leo X is attributed either to Pier Maria Serbaldi da Pescia, who was nicknamed 'Taglicacarne' because he was a pupil of the Genoese Giacomo Tagliacarne, or to his contemporary Michele Poggini, also called 'Michelino'. An interesting fact is that Giovanni delle Corniole subsequently had a pupil called Domenico di Polo who was to achieve fame as a counterfeiter of gems and the coins of antique medallions, and who worked in the time of Cosimo I.

Lorenzo the Magnificent took over the Government of Florence in 1469,[10] a year which marked the height of exuberance of the Renaissance, when he was little more than twenty years old. The first years of his rule in Florence formed a period of almost continuous feasting, art, music, poetry and enjoyment of life. This extraordinary prince, besides his duties of state and his work for the foundation of institutions for the increase of knowledge, as well as his literary enterprises, was, together with his brother Giuliano, invariably the organiser of the feasts. He was expert at arranging costly spectacles 'full of classical references and poetic allusions' for the diversion of his people. He wrote Latin verse and took part in the musical entertainments. Yet he did not neglect the duties of state, but on the contrary was a most successful administrator.

In the second half of the fifteenth century humanism and the effects of the great discoveries completely transformed society. The prosperity and power of Florence reached extraordinary heights, and the trade with the East became overwhelmingly important. These considerations explain the increasing importation of precious objects. After the death of Lorenzo's brother, Giuliano, assassinated during the Pazzi conspiracy, all feasting suddenly ceased. A further period of tranquillity lasted from 1480 until the end of his reign. In spite of difficulties he governed wisely; he did not even rage against Savona-

121

69 *Aron at the Tabernacle. Panel for the altar of the Princes' Chapel, after a design by Cigoli and Bilivert. It is made of Sicilian jasper, lapis lazuli, chalcedony and Bohemian jasper. Florence, Museo dell' Opificio.*

70 *Rectangular panel after a design by Cigoli and Bilivert. It is made of striped Sicilian jasper, 'flowered' Sicilian jasper, Bohemian jasper, lapis lazuli and chalcedony. Florence, Museo dell' Opificio.*

71 *Panel with floral motif. Decoration of lapis lazli, Volterra chalcedony, Sicilian jasper and German agate on a black background. Florence, Museo dell' Opificio.*

rola, whom, ironically, he himself had first called to Florence. A great friend of the arts, it is to him that we owe most of the important paintings and sculptures which are to be found in Florence today. He discovered Michelangelo and founded a school of sculpture in his garden; he gave a new impetus to the crafts of gemcutting and goldsmithing. His collection of art and precious objects was outstanding. In 1471 the Duke of Milan, Galeazzo Sforza, who was noted for his wealth, visited Florence with his wife, Bona of Savoy, and a large following to see Lorenzo and also to make a show of his riches. He failed in this latter object however, and at the end of his visit declared that he had never seen 'so many paintings by the greatest masters, statues, bronzes, gems, beautiful vases, medallions and rare books as he had seen collected in the Medici palace'.[11]

With the death of Lorenzo in 1492 and the brief reign of his son Pietro, nicknamed 'the unfortunate', came decadence. The Medicis were chased out of Florence in 1494, and popular fury destroyed or dispersed great numbers of precious things which had so carefully been collected over so many years. Many of the pieces that once belonged to the Medici are to be found in the museums of London, Paris, Naples, Vienna, Madrid and Leningrad. The precious vases bearing the initials of Lorenzo were rediscovered in 1502, and sent Leonardo into ecstasies. When they were rediscovered, the agate vase was valued at two hundred ducats. The jasper piece with the silver pedestal was valued at one hundred and fifty. Fifty years later they were sought out and bought by Cosimo I.

After the government of the Signoria, the Medicis returned to Florence with Giuliano, Duke of Nemours; meanwhile Europe was overwhelmed by political and religious strife and the exigencies of Lutheran reform. His brief reign ended in 1515 when the Duke Alessandro was sent to Florence by Giulio de Medici (later to become Clement VII), following the Treaty of Barcelona. The city suffered the consequences of this move, and Alessandro did nothing to increase the artistic patrimony. His tragic death in 1527, due to a further revolt, brought with it further dispersion of works of art. Alessandro was succeeded by Cosimo I, who was of the junior branch of the family and took the succession through lack of other heirs. He was a cruel man, but a thorough administrator, and he undertook great work on behalf of his domain. His patronage of the arts was on a grand scale, and within a short time he did much to rebuild the collection of his ancestors. After his death his eldest son, then a young man, was eventually consolidated in his position as legitimate successor, becoming Francesco I of Tuscany. He inherited from his father the taste for tyranny, and further nursed an almost obsessive passion for the sciences. His reign was marked by intrigues at Court, by family strife and by his own ill government; yet his inclination for the arts led him to found the *Accademia della Crusca*, which achieved in the shortest time a world-wide reputation, and also the Galleria degli Uffizi in the open gallery of the top floor of the building his father had intended as the seat of government. This bizarre prince was a dilettante and a refined collector, and spent much of his time in the so-called *Casino mediceo di San Marco* built by Buontalenti, where he experimented with anti-poisonous potions, botanical collections, the smelting of crystal, fireworks – and principally with the working of hard stones, an interest he seems to have acquired practically as an inherited characteristic. His first interest was jewellery, and in

72 *Panel with a sunflower. It is made of Sicilian jasper, Volterra jasper, and Sienese and German agate on a black background. Florence, Museo dell' Opificio.*

this he seems to have been a real connoisseur. He had the most beautiful pieces made, both genuine and counterfeit, by a Flemish craftsman called Jacopo Delfe (since his native city was Delft) and whose real name was Jacopo Bilivert. The latter came to the Medici service in 1573 from Augsburg in Germany, where he was already famous for his goldsmithing. Other Dutch and German masters came with him to Florence, and there made vases and goblets sometimes with animal friezes in rock crystal and usually with some mystery as to whether they were genuine or false. Other pieces were mounted in gold, or were made of gold and hard stones. Many of these were sent as gifts to fellow sovereigns, and their quality was such as to distinguish Florence even in the sumptuous midst of the 'triumph of European mannerism'. A number of them are still to be seen in the Palazzo Pitti, where they still show originality of design as well as the fine workmanship that first made them famous.

Zobi[12] quotes the following story from the Domenican Father Agostino del Riccio:

'I went to the City of Florence during the time of the reign of the Grand Duke Francesco and to where (the Casino of San Marco) he often went both in the mornings and after eating. He had gathered there men expert in all the arts and there were in the palace masters of every kind of gem working upon large and small vases and pieces in lapis lazuli. ... Also to be seen were masters of intaglio who were inlaying in a small stone a picture of the City of Florence, a work that I beheld with great content. It was little larger than a silver *scudo*. I also saw how another stone about the size of a large nut was being inlaid with an armed figure; there were many other such ingenious works in progress there. I saw for instance a cockerel made so small that it was difficult to make out all the pieces, for eagle eyes were needed to perceive all its parts.'

The famous Montaigne also met Francesco in Florence and wrote in the Journal of his Italian Journey: 'Car il est Prince souigneus un peu d'archemie et des arts méchaniques et surtout grand architecte'.[13]

Apart from availing himself of the services of the goldsmith, sculptor and architect Bernardo Buontalenti, Francesco brought to Florence – perhaps at the suggestion of the 'Venetian' Grand Duchess[14] – the Venetian artist Jacopo Ligozzi. He was to paint 'splendidly' plants and animals, and to collaborate on the grandiose scheme in hard stone for the Medici mausoleum of San Lorenzo, for which he was to train other craftsmen. Various artists were brought from Milan too to take part in this project, among them the inlayer Giovanni Bianchi.

Various quarrels blew up between these Milanese masters and the Florentine artists, for the latter, in spite of their reputations for learning quickly, took aversion to the prolonged presence of so many 'foreigners' in their City. In this connection there is an interesting letter conserved in the Medici archives, dated 22 September 1580, and sent from Cavaliere Giovanni Seriacopi to the Grand Duke. It recounts among other things how, when the writer went to the Casino di San Marco, he learned that 'the Milanese master Giorgio (Garuffi) and others simply play about and lock themselves in, putting bars across the entrance in such a way that no one can get in without their permission. And they do very little work. I must say at once to your Highness that if some action is not taken against the insolence of master Giorgio and his boy, they will get their heads chopped off; for they have already begun to

73 *Octogonal table by Ligozzi and Pocetti. Sicilian jasper, Volterra chalcedony, lapis lazuli and various types of agate on a black background. Florence, Museo dell' Opificio.*

fight with master Jacopo (Ligozzi), Your Highness's own painter who is in the Casino.'[15]

Now, four centuries later, one smiles at these squabbles between temperamental artists even as one admires the work that they produced and which is still unforgotten.

Zobi[16] mentions several pieces in *commesso* in the Charter-house at Pavia which can be dated to 1511; from this it is possible to argue that such work was produced in Lombardy before it was adopted in Florence, and it also explains the necessity for calling in the Milanese masters. Such work was made in Florence in the time of the Grand Duke Cosimo I, but it is clear that 'Florentine *commesso*' really developed under Francesco I as a prelude to the construction of the Medici Chapel. It is also clear that the development of the quality of the work owed a great deal to the skills of gem-cutting which had been practised for centuries under the Medicis.

Francesco died mysteriously after thirteen years of rule. The throne passed to his clever brother Ferdinando I, a cardinal of the Roman Curia whose character was very different to that of his predecessor. A peaceful, orderly man, he initiated a period of stable well-being such as Tuscany has perhaps never known since. He kept the best elements of his brother's eccentricities, and encouraged the craftsmen whom his brother had collected and trained.

As if in sanction of the aspirations of his forbears, on 3 September 1588 a solemn Grand Ducal Decree[17] formalised the position of the craftsmen of the Court and so founded the *Opificio delle Pietre Dure* which counted among its members such notable artists as Bernardo Buontalenti,[18] Matteo Nigetti,[19] Jacopo Ligozzi, Ludovico Cardo, nicknamed 'il Cigoli',[20] Jean Boulogne

74 *Detail of a large table in* commesso. *Florence, Palazzo Pitti, Museo degli Argenti.*

(Giambologna), Bernardino Barbatelli ('il Poccetti'), Jacopo Bilivert,[21] Pietro Tacca, Jacopo Autelli, Orazio Mochi, Francesco Mochi, and others.

Through these men the taste for coloured stones spread, and it was them who developed the art of making pictures which gave the illusion of perspective. This was the period of the late Renaissance, when the new research into figural expression that was tied to the interest in humanistic literature, the exaltation of colour and form and the taste for abundant decoration played an important part in the evolution of the art.

But the first need was to discover those colours which lay hidden in mountain tracks or river beds and to learn how to recognise boulders and pebbles, the shapeless exterior of which gave no hint of the fascinating qualities that the artist could extract from them. So many people wanted them that the Grand Duke Ferdinando offered prizes to those who found such materials and ordered punishments for anyone who wastefully scattered them. A curious decree on the subject reads as follows:[22] 'The most serene Grand Duke of Tuscany and the Respectable Members of the Guard Magistrate's Bench of the City of Florence, wishing to ensure that hard polishable stones are not mined except for the purpose of the ornament of Churches and Chapels to the honour of God, and so that they may be recorded and sent to other foreign States, have resolved, and by virtue of the present Proclamation ordered and commanded, that from the Vicariata of Scarperia, Firenzuola, and Palazzuolo, from the Postesteria of Barga, the Commessariato of Volterra, the Vicariato of Certaldo, or other mountainous parts of the State wheresoever are found or may be found in the future mines of polishable hard stones such as Jaspers, Agates, Chalcedonies and transparent Amethysts, coloured or similar, no one shall either use such stones for arquebus flints or break or smash them with hammers, or apply any other instrument to them or remove them beyond the boundaries of the State, under pain of punishment by fine of 50 scudi and ten years imprisonment.... Transgressors will be punished with the full rigour of the law without regard to any excuse. 10 July 1602, Donato Roffia, Chancellor.'

The Opificio commenced its brilliant career with the realisation of the long awaited Chapel which was indeed a triumph of *intarsio*, mosaic, tapestries, sculpture and rare hard stones; the whole exceeded the sober Tuscan tradition to assume an almost over luxurious atmosphere.

Zobi[23] quotes from the unpublished 'chronicle' of Settimanni[24] as follows:
'This day, 6 August 1604: The Most Serene Grand Duke [Ferdinando I] having selected a place near the Church of San Lorenzo where might be built a most sumptuous Chapel, at half past two o'clock on Friday morning of the Holy Passion of Our Lord, his Highness transferred himself there with all his Court, where he caused to be given to his first born son, Principe don Cosimo, a gilded mattock with which he dug into the ground at the point where the foundations were to be and brought out a quantity of earth, which he placed in a gilded basket with a gilded shovel; hence with this earth began the digging of the foundations and at the end of the ceremony the Grand Duke said: "Here will be our end".'

This is the text of one of the tablets of 1640 found walled into the foundations of the Chapel:[25]
'On 10 January were begun the foundations of this temple under the direction of Ferdi-

75 *Detail of a large table in* commesso *with a black background. Florence, Palazzo Pitti, Galleria Palatina.*

nando I, Grand Duke of Tuscany, who was succeeded by his son Cosimo, and then by Ferdinando II, the architect prince Don Giovanni Medici. The Grand Duke commanded the work of the Florentine architect Matteo Nigetti, who worked for the abovementioned prince, and who undertook the order to make designs and models both for the walls and for the jasper altar and ciborium of the most Holy Sacrament. So much has been undertaken of the work up to the present year 1640 and will be continued, thanks be to our God.'

In fact Buontalenti was the first to work at the project, and he was followed by Nigetti who worked at it until 1648, thus spending his life over a work that was 'imposing but requiring patience and an assiduous and slow achievement. It is said that years were required to incise each of the inscriptions upon the various sarcophagi, a labour that was not one of creation but rather of definition and execution, and each piece in the mausoleum is separated from the others by its particular character'.[26] At that time in the east wing on the first floor of the Uffizi Gallery a great crowd of people, among whom were to be found the best goldsmiths, sculptors and artists in general from various regions of Italy as well as from Germany and Flanders, worked towards the realisation of this dream.

It is interesting to notice that the structural walls of the Chapel were constructed rather slowly. Begun in 1604, in 1611 the fabric was completed to the point of the positioning of the arches, and '(only) that abutting upon the church was complete'. However alacrity characterised the realisation of the grandiose altar which was to exceed any other in magnificence and which was enriched by those intricate decorations that were to transform the traditionally severe Florentine altars towards the close of the sixteenth century (Plates 69, 70).

When Cigoli became designer of the Opificio in the early years of the seventeenth century, he was already involved in this colossal project which was, in fact, never finished, nor ever seen by anyone completed as originally intended. It is possible to acquire some conception of the tremendous labour that was undertaken by looking today at the pieces scattered among the altar of the church of San Lorenzo, the altar of the Palatine Chapel, the altar of the Chapel of the Villa del Poggio, the Museo degli Argenti, and the Museo dell' Opificio delle pietre dure. Not a single one of these became part of the later altar of the Chapel of the Princes.

Baldinucci[27] writes in his biography of Cigoli: 'The energy of the Grand Duke Ferdinando did much to speed up the work on the Chapel of San Lorenzo, according to the visions of his forbears; he was constantly adding new improvements so that, although it is today only half complete, it has achieved its original objective: namely, to be the most marvellous and noble thing of its kind to be seen in the entire world. When all that stupendous quantity and quality of hard and precious stone had been collected for the work and for the fine *commesso* that was continually executed by fine craftsmen in the Royal Gallery, he declared it to be his will that some way be found to use the material to make pictures in imitation of painting of certain sacred stories that would then be attached to the ciborium. When no one among these experts was forthcoming with the idea of how this should be done, he called our craftsman to him, who immediately understood the needs of his master and made according to his own ideas various beautiful designs, and thereafter spent five years among the masters

76 *Table top representing a view of the port of Leghorn. Sicilian and Bohemian jaspers, Sienese agate and Volterra chalcedony on a background of lapis lazuli. Florence, Palazzo Pitti, Museo degli Argenti.*

of the Royal Gallery instructing and assisting them in the production of these stupendous pictures of the stories that we see today.' The expression 'sacred stories' used by Baldinucci[28] is rather too general. Usually this is taken to mean either the 'Last Supper' and the 'Adoration of the Magi', which are to be seen today in the centre of the frontal of the great altar in San Lorenzo, or else those which were not used and are today in the Museo dell' Opificio. It seems likely that Cigoli produced all the cartoons for these sacred subjects, and that the differences which are noticeable between the pieces are the result of the various hands which actually worked to produce them.

These pieces are especially important in that they represent some of the first examples in which natural colour and patterns resulting from the various mineral contents have been patiently sought out and employed in *commesso* mosaic. This was done by cutting them into small single elements and matching them one against the other in a prearranged design, so as to obtain human figures and landscape backgrounds of surprising realism, the effects of which cannot be achieved by other means. In such cases it is impossible to think of the maker of these pieces as one who simply follows the design of a cartoon: the work must bear the stamp of an artist who has searched through the materials to find the piece that will achieve just the effect he desires. For example in Plate 76 the sky of the landscape is obtained by the use of a piece of golden Persian lapis lazuli, which has in it whitish calcium carbonate producing the effect of clouds. The outline of the hill, which so oddly recalls the brush-work of French eighteenth-century painters, is due to the naturally shaded Sicilian jaspers among which the red and green jaspers and the white

77 *Detail of a balustrade showing an inlay in* commesso *of hard stones. Agra, mausoleum of the Taj-Mahal.*

chalcedonies are realistically close in colour to the natural shades of trees and buildings. These then are the characteristics of the new art which was to overtake the process of refinement in the art of mosaics with which artists sought to represent the folds of robes or the minutiae of the human figure by means of the tiniest marble tesserae. Here, details are realised by exploiting the natural qualities of the materials, and thus the work must be defined as art rather than craftsmanship; and as an art of sufficient significance and scope to eschew the disparaging adjective 'minor' – an adjective wrongly used by critics in this connection. Whoever the artist may be – and it is difficult to attribute the pieces precisely either to Cigoli or to Bilivert in the absence of documentary evidence – his hand is evident both in the use of colour and the pictorial composition.

These are neither copies nor reproductions, and they are to be considered in the same light as canvases and frescoes. The landscape, 'David and the Lion', 'Abraham and the Angels', 'Aron at the Tabernacle' (Plate 69) and 'Jonah and the Whale' all have in common extraordinary chromatic and expressive power. The term miniature has been used for this work because the effects of detail are obtained by almost microscopic means. Where the stone is not actually used, the eye or a wrinkle or the lines of the hand are realised by tiny incisions. The incisions are then filled with a specially hard gum mastic that may be polished to a high brilliance. To be noted also are the vestments outlined with gold sequins which add opulence to the whole work.

These pieces have been examined in some detail because, although they are contemporary with other works, they represent a new departure from symbolic and floral decorations into the realms of descriptive art. Among the few attempts at portrait art must be mentioned the life-size half bust of the Grand Duke Cosimo I made by the sculptor and mosaicist Francesco Ferrucci in 1598, which, however, is a copy of the painting on canvas by Domenico Passignano painted a year earlier in 1597. The work is technically competent, but it could have been better in some respects. For variety of material and richness of design and colour the great table[29] designed and made by Jacopo Ligozzi and Bernadino Barbatelli, called Poccetti, for Ferdinando II certainly ranks amongst the most outstanding. Zobi[30] describes it as follows: 'The octagonal table (Plate 73) so highly and justly praised by Baldinucci has been moved from the Tribuna into the Sala del Baroccio in the Fiorentina Gallery. It is perhaps the largest piece to come out of the Granducal establishment, since it has a diameter of three and a half yards. Into a background of Flemish touch-stone are inlaid grotesque figures with shells, flowers, leaves, pearls and fish, all worked in *commesso* with agate, chalcedony, various jaspers and lapis lazuli. The design is that of Jacopo Ligozzi (according to Baldinucci) and the piece was also executed by him, apart from the central disc which would appear to be the work of Poccetti. It is surrounded by eight seashells which enclose as many dolphins entwined in pairs by their curling tails. At the centre a garland of oak leaves surrounds a globe of lapis lazuli, within which are three lilies of yellow jasper.

The beauty and richness of the stone makes this table superior to any other, although later pieces were made with more scrupulous accuracy and skill.'

This description illustrates how at the beginning of the seventeenth century the germ of Baroque appeared also in this art, and

78 *Wall of the Centaur and Parrot, in the Florentiner Zimmer, palace of the 'Favorite', Rastatt. Many of the small panels in hard stones have duplicates in the Museo dell' Opificio in Florence.*

began with the work of Poccetti, noted for his transformation of the so-called Florentine mannerism into a lively, spontaneous and rich design made of curls and grotesques crowded into a small space which, however, have a lively glitter of colour well suited to the medium of variegated stone.

Almost all the stones used here are hard except for the black background which is soft in relation to the others. In contrast with the work of Cigoli and Bilivert, the craftsmen have aimed only at a spectacular effect and have resorted to rather banal tricks to emphasize this: for example, hemispheres of rock crystals have been laid into the marble by the technique of *intarsio*, with the flat side uppermost, so as to produce the odd illusion that they are in relief. The vivid Florentine lilies are made of red jasper and contrast with the green oak fronds standing out at the base. The cream-coloured Volterra chalcedonies woven everywhere in the borders and intricate cornices dominate the black, and the tulips and yellow narcissi appear right across the surface in every available space with a virtuosity that almost exhausts the beholder. The piece required sixteen years of work on the part of a group of artists: it was begun in 1633 and finished in 1649.

Baldinucci[31] writes:
'The principal master was Jacopo Autelli, nicknamed 'Monnicca', assisted by Giovanni Merlini, Giovanni Giachetti, Giovanni Francesco Bottini, Giovanni Bianchi Juniore, Lorenzo Bottini, Cosimo Chermer, Giovanni Giorgi and Carlo Centelli. Those who cut the material were Pietro Chiari (called 'il Chimico') and Andrea Merlini; the polishers were Benedetto Celli and Pietro Cozzi. There were a further ten cutters who sawed at their work for the whole period it took to make the piece. The designer was the diligent painter Jacopo Ligozzi (who died in 1627), while the central *tondo* was designed by Bernadino Poccetti, another well-known painter. After the craftsman's death, Baccio del Bianco also had a part in it and advice was given by the engineers approved by the Most Serene Prince, then Cardinal Leopold of Tuscany.'

The quotation shows what solemnity attended the making of these pieces: while the work was, in the case of the table, that of craftsmen, the labour involved was immense and required consultation with the engineers and with the Prince of Tuscany himself. Yet this is but one of a very large number of tables manufactured during the period and sent as gifts to the leading personalities of Europe. Zobi[32] mentions that, in the reign of Ferdinand II, the Opificio acquired such fame that Florentine artists were in demand abroad; one of them, Ferdinando Migliorini, went to France to teach the art, although it seems that he had little success. Instead, during the reign of Cosimo III (1670–1723), another 'Opificio' was established at Naples[33] which was to enjoy a prosperous career for over one hundred years. The first workers to be sent there from Florence were Giovanni Battista Zucconi and Raffaello Muffati; Filippo Violi, Francesco Campi and Giuseppe Minchioni followed them at the beginning of the rule of Gian Gastone (1723–37). There were altars also in Naples, made of hard stone of both *commesso* and *intarsio* work, although they lacked the precision of the Florentine work. A truly imposing piece is in the church of the Charter-house of San Martino (mentioned in chapter II) where the whole pavement of the nave, presbytery and chapel are made in *commesso* of coloured marble, which has an amazing richness reminiscent of Spanish work and is impressive also by its very size. The whole church has motifs in *intarsio* and

79 *Wall with a glass trellis in which are painted portrait miniatures similar to those of the Uffizi in Florence. Rastatt, Palace of the 'Favorite'.*

commesso in the principal baluster, in the altar, and in the minor balusters of the chapels. Some hard and semi-precious stones, such as lapis lazuli, are also used.

There is little modern reference on the studio of Naples;[34] what there is shows little agreement with Zobi over such matters as the date of the institution and names of the Florentine artists who worked there.

Celano[35] has this to say about the Parthenopean Institute:

'Little thought of and little visited is the laboratory of hard stone, not because it is far away or high up, but because few people know of it. Yet amongst those institutions with which King Charles III enriched our city, this establishment must nonetheless be numbered. It is modelled on the Florentine one, and its work consists of reducing stones to various shapes and placing them together even though they may be very hard, so that they represent a picture of some kind that may serve as an ornament.

'In 1738 that magnanimous Prince sent to us from the metropolis of Tuscany ten of their most expert artists, among whom was the famous *intagliatore* Francesco Ghinghi, who was their director. They were housed in a suitable building, and provided with a rich stock of stone and the tools and instruments necessary, on the same site as it is to be found today, near the church of San Carlo alle Mortelle.

'It was intended first and foremost that they should work on the projects of the *Real Casa;* the altar in the chapel in the Royal Palace of Caserta together with other works in oriental granite were our first assignments, also the tabernacle for the same altar which is one of the richest and noblest to be seen, being formed of amethyst, lapis lazuli, petrified wood, granites, cornelians, agates and jaspers

80 *Another wall with glass trellis. Rastatt, Palace of the 'Favorite'.*

of wonderful beauty; equally wonderful are two topazes worked as bas-relief, and which serve as doors to two ciborii: these bas-reliefs represent an effigy of the Redeemer. The two topazes were originally a single piece weighing eleven and a half pounds, and have been reduced to less than a hand's breadth.'

81 *Detail of wall showing panels in hard stones and panels in stucco. Rastatt, Palace of the 'Favorite'.*

82 *Overleaf: Table top with* commesso *panels on a black background. The table undoubtedly came from Florence. Rastatt, Palace of the 'Favorite'.*

'With the passage of time the old masters disappeared and political circumstances also conspired to reduce their numbers, until Francesco I conceived the idea of reviving the Opificio in all its ancient splendour. In 1828, Signor Orazio Angelini was therefore sent to Florence to study and acquire mastery in all aspects of the art. His task was to cut and polish the ancient stones that had been found, and to train other artists as well.

'As a result of the royal determination and of successive gifts, the offices of the Opificio have completed a considerable number of successful works. The stores of tools and stones are full and in good order; among the latter is a piece which is perhaps unique: a mass of eastern petrified wood almost circular in form and 8·75 of a hand's breadth in diameter, made of red onyx, clacedony and agate, the whole being a slice from a tree trunk showing the concentric rings.

'It is known that this massive piece of material was found abandoned on the *Molo* of this city but no one has been able to discover where it came from or who put it there. A large part of it has already been incorporated in various works.

'Today the Opificio consists of a director who is also chief designer, a manager, a first master, two under-masters and various pupil sawsmen who are maintained by the Royal Treasury, and have besides free accommodation in the above-mentioned building.'

Other references are furnished by Giovanni Tescione.[36] He gives the date of the foundation of the institute as 1738 and of its closing as 5 March 1861. Above all he mentions the most important work entrusted to it: the altar and tabernacle of the Palatine Chapel.

The work of the Opificio at Naples gains significance if it is considered in relation to that of similar institutions, such as the one at Leghorn founded by Ferdinando I in 1601 as the *Fabbrica delle Pietre Dure* and directed by Bernardino Gaffurri. Although this studio had a short life in comparison with the one in Florence, it testifies once again to the fervent activity with which the art was then pursued.

To return to the end of the seventeenth century when the Grand Duke Cosimo III (1642–1723) reigned in Tuscany, having succeeded his father Ferdinando II in 1670: this monarch is throughly denigrated by Young,[37] who describes him as 'vacuous, weak, tyrannical, brainless, superstitious and bigoted', and defines his long reign as characterised by physical and moral ills. He occupied himself much with his family mausoleum and had it rearranged, but he found himself on the throne during a critical period for Europe. For almost twenty years the war between France, Spain and Austria had menaced the independence of Tuscany. In the midst of chaos, Cosimo contrived to lend consideration to the arts and to the running of the Opificio. In 1697 he sent Florentine artists to Goa[38] to decorate the tomb of St Francis Xavier, and in this connection Zobi[39] quotes the following letter written by Cosimo to Father Xavier de Almeyda, Provincial of the Jesuits there:

'In consideration of the signal grace God has shown me in allowing me to have some connection with His glorious Apostle of the Indies, St Francis Xavier, I have thought to contribute something which might ornament the tomb of the saint, and which records the finest acts of his holy life sculptured in bronze.'

Zobi further recounts that two young craftsmen, Giuseppe Ramponi and Marco Fanciullacci, were sent to Goa to 'mount the foundation of the venerable remains. They returned to Florence by way of Lisbon after some years'.

83 *Detail of preceding, round panel in* commesso *with a landscape.*

84 *Tondo in* commesso, *showing a landscape with a river. It is made of oriental alabaster, Sicilian jasper, lapis lazuli, chalcedony and other stones. Florence, Museo dell' Opificio.*

Zobi's wish is to demonstrate that these two, during their stay in India, taught the art of working hard stone, and that the decoration of the Taj-Mahal was the fruit of their instruction. Bussagli[40] writes: 'This symbol of Moghul India, this architectural chef d'oeuvre which has inspired poets and writers of every period and every land, is in reality a mausoleum, the sumptuous tomb of a queen, Arjumand Banu Begum, wife of the Emperor Shah Jahan, and better known by the epithets (which are proper court titles in the complicated ceremonial of the Moghuls) of Mumtaz Mahal (the preferred of the palace) or Taj-Mahal (the diadem of the palace – which means really of the empire).' The author narrates the misfortunes of this unhappy queen, and tells how her consort never ceased to grieve after her death and made for her a marvellous construction of what she herself had seen in a dream a little before her death: 'A wonderful palace of carved white marble and before it a splendid garden with gurgling fountains.'

The monument stands today at Agra on the right bank of the river Jumna. Its construction was begun in 1632 and completed in 1648. Bussagli states that 'it is therefore very probable that the artist – or at least one of the artists – was a European so profoundly versed in the western pictorial tradition as to be able to capture the fabulous and unreal

85 *Panel with a parrot, made of lapis lazuli, chalcedony and jaspers. Florence, Museo dell' Opificio.*

86 *Detail of a parrot very similar to the one shown on the preceding photograph. Rastatt, Palace of the 'Favorite'.*

feeling of the buildings which he had seen reproduced in miniatures and from which he took his inspiration. Clearly he must have been versed in architectural and decorative techniques, since he was able to achieve a total and complicated effect of illusion as to colours, materials and proportions. And the only person who possessed these qualities and who worked on the Taj-Mahal was the Venetian Geronimo Veroneo.'

Further on, the same author writes: 'As for the other decorations, which are rather sober and cover only limited areas of the building, they are generally in the form of bunches of grapes, bouquets of flowers, fruits and birds which show little variation (or perhaps one should say show frequent repetition of the same motif), and they are made in hard stones with occasional insertions of precious stones. The motifs are not original since similar work is to be found in the famous tomb of Itimad ud-Daulah, and also in some Persian and Moghul miniatures where certain architectural structures are finely reproduced. The choice of hard stone for use in decoration is specified in various texts, and with particular precision in a manuscript preserved in the Bibliothèque Nationale in Paris. Lapis lazuli, various kinds of jasper, agate, cornelian, jade and amethyst together with yellow and black marble, onyx and mediterranean coral were all used. Here and there

87 *Sketch painted on canvas by Giuseppe Zocchi for the series of* commesso *panels representing the seasons. Florence, Museo dell' Opificio.*

precious stones were inlaid (brilliants, emeralds, and sapphires) but most of these were removed by the Afghan soldiers of Ahmed Shah Durani after the tragic battle of Panipat (13 January 1761).'

It is interesting to note that the technique both of *commesso* and *intarsio* is the same as that employed during the period in the Opificio of hard stones; and furthermore that the quality of the jaspers and other stones is very similar to that of those to be seen in the museum at Florence (Plate 77). There are also baroque-like motifs to be observed in the leaves and vases that have been depicted, as well as local oriental motifs that are not found in Europe. Certainly there are strict parallels with contemporary work from the Opificio which are hard to explain except as the result of direct influence either from or upon the Florentine workers.

The hypothesis of Zobi would be acceptable were it not for dating, for it is very possible that the decorations of the building were made considerably later than the structure. However Bussagli's well-founded hypothesis upon the intervention of an Italian, and in particular of a Venetian, in the building of the Taj-Mahal in no way excludes the possibility that Florentines may have taught the Indian artists who produced the work in hard stone, which would fall in the period of the highest activity of the Tuscan Institute.

88 *A musical scene, by Zocchi. It is made of oriental onyx, Sicilian and Bohemian jaspers, lapis lazuli and chalcedony. Florence, Museo dell' Opificio.*

The construction and especially the decoration of this astonishing palace in India has fascinated many writers, among them G. F. Young, who writes in the chapter in which he narrates the life of Ferdinando II, son of Cosimo II:[41]

'It is precisely in the Taj that one sees for the first time the change in the style of *intarsio* that denotes the influence of Florentine artists – a change which is even more pronounced in the *intarsi* that decorate the palaces at Delhi and Agra. In 1648 Ferdinand (who was probably put in contact with the Moghul emperor by the Augustinian brethren in India), with the intention of further perfecting the new Florentine industry, sent Austin of Bordeaux, a Frenchman in his service and one of the principal craftsmen of the Royal Opificium and some companions to the Emperor Shah Jahan to obtain certain silicates that were to be found only in India. The Florentines, while they were at the Court of the Grand Moghul, suggested designs for the inlays which were to decorate the new palaces at Delhi and Agra, introducing particularly delicate floral motifs into them. Austin of Bordeaux himself decided not to leave India, and instead entered the permanent service of the Emperor Shah Jahan. In this capacity he was responsible for the ornamentation of the Palace at Delhi and for the construction of the Peacock Throne. Austin of Bordeaux was

89 *Sketch of the Pantheon, by Ferdinando Partini. Florence, Museo dell' Opificio.*

later poisoned by some person who was jealous of his influence over the emperor.

'This is how the *intarsio* at Delhi and Agra came to bear resemblance to the Florentine work that we have mentioned. Thus it was that Tuscany, even in the time of decadence, was able to influence work in lands far beyond its own narrow borders, and to leave its mark upon one of the most beautiful arts of India.'

Bernard Taylor was probably Young's source for all this information, and it is comforting that it has at last become possible to envisage a complete picture of the Tuscan origin of these works.

It was also during the reign of Cosimo III that the Opificio was entrusted with a work that has been undervalued and indeed almost forgotten both by critics and recent historians. This consists of a fine collection of *commessi* in hard stone of exquisite workmanship and high quality, which may be admired in the so-called palace of the 'Favorite', in the little German city of Rastatt in the Baden district to the south of Karlsruhe. This was the seat of the Margraves of Baden-Baden, and its importance lies in the political events that occurred there. Among other things it was there that the negotiations took place between France and the Emperor Charles VI in 1714, at the end of the war of the Spanish Succession, and there also that the inter-European congress was held after the Treaty of Campoformio, which in 1798 ceded the left bank of the Rhine to France.

With this city was bound the life of the Margravine Sibylla Augusta (1675–1733), a beautiful and talented woman who, a few years after the death of her husband, the Margrave Louis-William of Baden-Baden, decided to continue the building of the new palace known as the 'Favorite' The life of

90 Commesso *panel of the Pantheon, made of European and oriental chalcedony, jaspers, petrified wood and lapis lazuli. Florence, Museo dell' Opificio.*

this powerful woman was eventful and difficult, and after her death legends grew up around her, suggested perhaps initially by the epigraph she ordered for herself: 'Pray for this great sinner'. Round this an infinity of strange stories collected, most of which were utterly without foundation.

The truth in fact was that Sibylla Augusta, born in Saxe-Lauenburg, married a General who became famous and was nicknamed 'Türkenlouis', after a resounding victory he had gained over the Turks. He himself was Prince Regent of a small country weakened by a lengthy war, and which depended upon its leader making a rich marriage in order to survive. The Emperor Leopoldo I therefore gave his lieutenant one of the richest heiresses of the time: the fifteen-year-old Sibylla Augusta, who found herself immediately plunged into the diplomacy of south-western Germany, following her husband from one encampment to the next. 'Türkenlouis' had a distinguished pupil in Eugene of Savoy, famous for his tactics and for his talent as a condottiere. The former died in 1707 of an incurable wound, after beginning work on the Palace of Rastatt which he was not to see completed. Sibylla was thus, while still young, the regent of a country which had been much wasted by war and which became to her a second homeland, until such time as her son, later called 'Louis the hunter', grew to manhood. This shrewd woman possessed a powerful will and governed with unforeseen skill, at the same time caring for the two sons and one daughter who had survived out of the nine to whom she had given birth.

Her character showed many facets, which were the result of her wealthy childhood on the one hand, and her hard adult life on the other. She was both modest and religious, yet she also had a passionate temperament and loved luxury. During the twenty long years of her regency, she brought prosperity to her adopted land, partly by use of her Bohemian fortune. Her father, Duke Julius Francis, had built the castle of Schlackenwerth, where in 1673 a collection of art and curios was placed in a pavilion, according to the fashion of the period. Here Sibylla had lived with her elder sister Anna Maria Francesca until the early death of her parents. This was a splendid world that she remembered always with great nostalgia and which gave her an exquisite sensitivity which remained with her all her life. When the castle at Baden-Baden was destroyed by the French, she and 'Türkenlouis' moved back to Schlackenwerth and it is no wonder that the new palace and garden of the 'Favorite' was built upon this model.

The project of the new residence began to take shape while Sibylla was staying in Bohemia in about 1710. She entrusted the execution of the scheme to her young compatriot, Michael Ludwig Rohrer (1683–1732), in the year 1707, after she had sent away the Italian architect Domenico Egidio Rossi, whom 'Türkenlouis' had brought from Vienna to build the residential Castle of Rastatt. Sibylla placed Rohrer in charge of all the official construction work, for his father had directed all the works undertaken by the Margrave, and had even accompanied him in his campaigns. The same family was also to produce Peter Ernest Rohrer, who later entered the service of the Margravine. Numerous artists were invited to take part in the building of the 'Favorite': many came from Bohemia and stayed there to work under the direction of the Rohrers.

Sibylla allowed no one to waste time and insisted upon a rapid completion of the work: building continued even through the hard winter until May 1711, when all the wooden

91 *Table top of Florentine* commesso *work. It is made of Volterra chalcedony, lapis lazuli, jasper, German and Goan agate on a background of nephrite. Florence, Palazzo Pitti.*

92 The 'Table of the Muses', after a design by G. B. Giorgi, made of chalcedony, Goan agate, Alsatian and Sicilian jaspers on a background of lapis lazuli. Florence, Palazzo Pitti, Galleria Palatina.

framework was completed, and by the following winter the roof was on. The interior, however, required much refined and painstaking labour and was not finished until many years later. It was decorated by another Italian: the painter Michele Sanguinetti. The furnishing of the whole building was entrusted to the painter Franz Pfleger, who had worked under the architect Rossi as a designer for the castle. His influence was considerable, and so thoroughly did he gain Sibylla's confidence that she would refer to him as 'my dear Franz'.

By 1720 the greater part of the work was completed, and during the last years of her life Sibylla – now an old woman – occupied herself with certain details of refinement. In 1729, J. C. Keyssler observed that of the numerous works of *intarsio* and *commesso* that were intended to figure in the so-called 'Florentiner Zimmer' (Plate 78) only one table was completed. But Sibylla renounced the regency in 1727 in favour of the hereditary Prince Lüdwig George, and came less and less often to the 'Favorite', although it had been the principal object of her life. It is interesting that a new family connection arose between the Medici and the Margravine Sibylla when, in 1697, the Grand Duke Gian Gastone married Anna Maria of Saxe-Lauenburg, elder sister of Sibylla. Gian Gastone was only twenty-four and it seems likely that the marriage took place partly for financial reasons and perhaps also partly with the object of obtaining certain mining rights. Anna Maria had inherited her wealth from her father, who had left no male heirs, and her own husband, who had died. She is said to have been 'a most impressive person',[43] authoritarian, ill-tempered, dedicated to hunting and outdoor life. Gian Gastone, whose character was entirely different and whose health was precarious, lived with her only out of duty; he finally abandoned her and was separated from her in 1708.

With the death of the Margravine Sibylla in 1733 some changes took place at the 'Favorite' and some superfluous furniture was removed. Then silence descended again and only Lüdwig paid occasional visits there until he died in 1761. August Georg succeeded to the Margravate and, at his death in 1771, it was combined with that of Baden Durlach. The 'Favorite' passed to Charles Frederick who made certain changes there and resided at Karlsruhe. Petrasch[44] comments that 'a generous fate has left this magnificent place to us almost intact'. Thus it was that the 'Florentiner Zimmer' was never finished, and the *Opificio fiorentino* was entrusted with the furnishing of all the decoration in hard stone. The Palace itself is filled with decorated paving, tapestries, embroideries, inlays of mother-of-pearl and fine mirrors (Plates 79, 80, 81).

The 'Florentiner Zimmer' was never completed and much *commesso* was replaced by inferior painting on glass or painted stucco. On the other hand, in the museum of the Opificio at Florence are to be found numerous small panels (Plates 84, 85, 86) which closely resemble those that decorate the walls at Rastatt, and which must surely either be faithful replicas of the originals or else unsuccessful pieces which were kept in Florence – unless they were pieces which were simply never sent to their destination. In particular a series of *tondi* showing various lansdcapes in hard stone are strangely similar both in dimensions and in form to those at Rastatt; these latter however are very often simply in painted glass (Plates 82, 83). These pieces cannot be of other provenance than Florence, since *commesso* work was then at its height in that city, while the family connection between the Grand Duke and the Margravine seems to leave no doubts upon the subject.

The room at Rastatt is a late example of the fashion for possessing objects in hard stone which had become almost a family tradition with the Medicis. These decorations in circles, rectangles and squares with leafy and floral motifs, small landscapes, animal or grotesque compositions mixed with mythological scenes occupy the entire wall space, except where a space must be left for doors and windows. Famous motifs are continually repeated, and exact replicas of them are to be seen in the museum at Florence. During the years of the internal decoration of Rastatt, one of the principal workers at the Opificio was Antonio Torricelli. From Fiesole, he was the founder of a family of artists who made amongst other things the portrait of Ferdinando II in *commesso* and wrote a tract upon hard stones and the methods of working them in 1714. He was an energetic man, and possessed great ingenuity in the making of the strangest objects in hard stone. He was, however, by no means modest; Zobi[45] records some of his remarks about his own work as follows: 'I have also made glasses, beakers, cups and snuff boxes tightened with screws, and am myself the inventor of the method of screwing up hard stone, and it would be difficult for me to recount all the things I have done with chains and wheels and so on.' When he died in 1719, his son Gaetano and then his nephew Giuseppe followed him in his work at the Opificio. At the beginning of the eighteenth century, the triumph of *commesso* and gemcutting continued in the work of Giovan Battista Foggini, who was a skilful sculptor. One of his most significant works is the altar of the Madonna all'Impruneta near Florence which, together with the beaten silver frontal, is a fine example of the kind of

93 *Panel decorating the altar, after a design by G. B. Giorgi. It is made of lapis lazuli, chalcedony, Volterra and Sicilian jaspers, Arno jasper and petrified wood. Florence, Basilica of S. Lorenzo, Princes' Chapel.*

94 *Curved table top made of petrified wood, lapis lazuli, Sabine and Goan agate, Volterra chalcedony, Sicilian, Cypriot and Alsatian jaspers and amethyst quartz. Florence, Museo dell' Opificio.*

work that was done during this epoch of lace and embroidery, when the luxury of the clothes of the Grand Dukes and the candid and ephemeral stucco architecture served to hide from the people the decadence of their minds.

As all worldly things, the family of the Medici came to an end, and one cannot but agree with Young[46] when he writes: 'While other rulers of that time left nothing except the memory of their personal glory, which itself is soon cancelled by time, the Medici left behind them things that will endure.' Their great achievement was to increase knowledge, to encourage all the arts and artists so that the world possesses far more treasures than it would have done without them, and for this we must be grateful to them in spite of the human failings they displayed.

On 9 July 1737, at the death of the Grand Duke Gian Gastone, his sister, the Electoress Anna Maria (Luisa) Ludovica, was seventy years old; she had married, at the age of twenty-four, William, Elector Palatine of the Rhine. Her brother's last days had been embittered by the failure of his marriage and an illness of the brain, and had been spent in dissolution. The government was disorganised and weak. Her own marriage with the Elector had proved itself unhappy and, when she was widowed at the age of fifty in 1716, she continued her existence in modest retirement, concerning herself with charitable work and with the collection of art, which she generously left to Florence when she died in 1743. In this immense collection there are mosaics, cabinets and other furniture decorated with gold and silver, and vases in hard stone which are today in the Palazzo Pitti and the museum of the Opificio (Plates 74, 75, 76).

Thus closes on a rather sad note this chapter of the story of Florence which gradually involved Tuscany, the whole of Italy and the rest of Europe. Tuscany now passed into very different hands: Francis, Duke of Lorraine, who was too busy with the affairs of his own country, nominated a council of men to act as regents, under the leadership of a man called Beauveau, upon whom he conferred the titles of Prince of Craon and Count of Richecourt. The Duke himself remained at Vienna with his consort Maria Teresa, in expectation of the imperial title that was conferred upon him in 1745.

Meanwhile, the Opificio of hard stones continued its work, maintained as always by the state. In 1749 the Frenchman Louis Siries was nominated Director. He was born at Figeac in Quercy, and went to Florence from the Court of Louis XV in 1722.

Louis Siries availed himself of the talents of a Florentine painter of unusual merit, Giuseppe Zocchi,[47] and desired him to make the designs and models for pictures in hard stone, upon subjects suggested by himself. These were of great variety, rather curious and full of figures; they succeeded remarkably well and were placed among the most prized and rarest objects in the Imperial Gallery in Vienna.

Sixty-one panels were made after Zocchi's paintings, together with two little tables in the Palazzo Pitti, one of which is decorated with shells and other marine subjects upon a background of lapis lazuli, while the other has butterflies and flowers of surprising delicacy upon a background of oriental alabaster. These works were completed in 1748 under the direction of Louis and Cosimo Siries, father and son, who interpreted the designs of the well-known painters Giuseppe Zocchi and Giovan Battista Iacopucci.[48]

In this connection it may be said that Zocchi shows the signs of two chief influences:

95 *Decorative panel made of oriental onyx, Volterra chalcedony, green jasper and Arno jasper. Florence, Museo dell' Opificio.*

one is the pictorial landscape favoured by many Venetian painters, and closely resembling the work of the Swiss Joseph Wagner, whose pupil he had been in Venice; and the other is owed to the reawakening of conscience urged by literary critics of the period. An entire series of paintings by Zocchi is in fact devoted to the daily life of a lady, always richly dressed, who figures at the centre of the attention of courtiers and sycophants, in the midst of games, dinners and receptions. Other pictures illustrate the games of children in various amusing attitudes, while others again describe military life, or move into allegories where landscapes are unreal and perspectives altered to lend giant size to proportions. One series illustrates the four liberal arts: music, painting, architecture and sculpture, all minutely and finely displayed with an abundance of beautifully inlaid alabaster, onyx and highly coloured jasper. Beside them, the oil paintings that served as models seem vague and dim (Plates 87, 88). The Opificio found itself faced with an impressive quantity of work that required a large staff of skilled workers to cope with it.

Zocchi, helped by Antonio Cioci and his son Leopoldo, gave the best of himself in his efforts to seek out colours which, when polished, had a liveliness that his canvases did not possess. With him, *commesso* became an art again, and certainly the labour required to produce such effects must have been prodigious. The clothes, draperies and architecture of the seventeenth century lent themselves easily to such composition. They have been reproduced in stones remarkably carefully worked. Effects of light and shade and perspective have been attentively studied – and great technical skill has gone into these features of the work, since they require the use of alternately hard and softer stones, which necessitates immensely careful craftsmanship. The oriental alabasters used to reproduce cloudy skies or window-panes; lapis lazuli which lends itself so well to imitating the rich materials of feminine dress; jasper which can be made to look like velvet: all these stones need to be handled by an experienced artist so as not to risk spoiling the ensemble with violent splashes of colour.

This is craftsmanship, indeed, but it is also art. The figures and the buildings still have a surprising brilliance which makes them fresh and vital. Only four of these marvellous pieces are exhibited in the Museum of the Opificio; they are not originals, but are instead late eighteenth-century copies, although finely done. To comprehend the value of the original work, it is sufficient to recall that these lively pieces were produced in a new manner during a period of dull, neo-classical mannerism in painting.

Zocchi's work in these respects was truly great; it seems certain that he did not limit his contribution to the drawing of the numerous models, but also helped in the transformation of his ideas into the indelible colours of stone. It is not known how many works were sent abroad apart from those which may today be seen in museums, but certainly the friendship and patronage of the imperial house of Austria must have encouraged a formidable export from the Opificio – the scale of this may be guessed from the vast quantity of works which still exist in the Florentine Institute.

The energetic imagination of Louis Siries[49] led him in 1794 to suggest to the Grand Duke Pietro Leopoldo that a 'room of hard stone' might be made at the Palazzo Pitti similar to the one already in existence at the Hofburg in Vienna, and he proposed a group of views of ancient buildings as the first series of works

166

96 *Console table top in* commesso *work, with borders decorated with musical instruments similar to those on contemporary Emilian pictures. Madrid, Prado, Tiepolo Room.*

to be incorporated in it. To this end, he sent a model of the Pantheon to the Palace, which was approved, begun at once and finished in 1797. In the museum are to be seen five other views of ancient Roman buildings. These were painted by Ferdinando Partini between 1794 and 1797 (Plates 89, 90), and some of them, like the one of the Temple of Janus, were removed by the French early in the nineteenth century and thus were dispersed.

Louis Siries was succeeded by his son Cosimo, who received special sponsorship from the Emperor and Grand Duke Francis[50] in Vienna on 21 June 1759. Cosimo remained in the post until his death in 1789. Another member of this family was then nominated: Louis Siries Junior, son of Cosimo, and the long succession concluded under the reign of Ferdinando II of Lorraine with Carlo Siries, son of Louis, nominated in 1812.

The dynasty of the Siries signalled another fine period of activity during which collaboration was made with many fine Florentine artists, among whom figured Antonio Cioci, Leopoldo Cioci and Giovan Battista Giorgi.

Commesso designs of landscapes and 'views' continued to be made in considerable numbers even after Zocchi was no longer on the scene. Antonio Cioci, a fine designer, made idealised versions of views of the port of Leghorn which were sent to Vienna as gifts from the Grand Duke Leopoldo of Lorraine to Prince Metternich. Antonio Cioci's son Leopoldo followed his father into the Opificio. He made a particularly fine table using nephrite – a stone which was employed only subsequent to the discovery of America, and which then became increasingly popular; its odd name refers to its reputation as a specific cure of kidney diseases. It is quite hard, and shows an almost black background lightly speckled with greenish-yellow markings. Cioci

167

97 *Console table top in* commesso *work similar in design to the panels made in Florence by G. Zocchi. Madrid, Prado. Tiepolo Room.*

inlaid into a panel of this material a series of scenes of the most lively colours and effect showing various porcelain vases (Plate 91). The excellence of the design and workmanship and the naturalness of the colour obtained by the means of small pieces of jasper, chalcedony and lapis lazuli combine to make this piece a work of art as well as of craftsmanship. The stems of flowering geranium, roses and convolvulus lend a pictorial liveliness to the composition which is totally different from the contemporary still-lives on canvas. These panels of Cioci, with their indelible and spectacular colours, realise the ancient dreams of the mosaicists who hankered after just such 'eternal pictures'.

Another famous designer who worked under Carlo, the last of the Siries, was Giovan Battista Giorgi. But times had changed, and with them the exigencies of art; 1789 brought the French Revolution that led towards the Napoleonic era and hence radical changes of custom. Finally, with the Empire, came the flowering of classical reminiscence in artistic taste. The naturalism so dear to Zocchi and his successors was abandoned in favour of the methodically ornate neo-classical designs and the stereotyped production of mythological scenes, still-lives, flowers, fruits and musical instruments. The qualities of such work consist of a craftsman-like virtuosity – lifeless and very different in spirit from the achievements of the previous century.

In 1796 Ferdinando III of Lorraine transferred the Opificio from the site in Via del Cocomero (now Via Ricasoli) to the suppressed convent of San Niccolo, where it is still located. Then came the period of the Bourbon regency, and with it the reputation of the Opificio increased to the point where it was granted a monopoly by a degree[51] from the Queen Regent on 11 June, 1806. Under

98 *Table top in* commesso *work of Florentine origin. Vienna, Kunsthistorisches Museum.*

its terms, it was 'prohibited to any person of whatever condition, grade or state, to make on his own account outside the same Opificio any *commesso* in hard stone or to sell similar work not acquired by the Royal Offices . . . upon pain of a fine of 300 scudi for each transgression'.

Thus the importance of this art was once again recognised, and work continued to appear throughout the nineteenth century that was of the most varied nature, and that included such pieces as the so-called 'table of the Muses' – an excellent piece of neo-classical work which is almost two metres in diameter (Plate 92). Among the materials used in it is a marvellous piece of lapis lazuli, the workmanship of which is of the finest quality. Designed by Giorgi, it remains a supreme example of craftsmanship which must have required years of patient skill in its execution. The differences of style however, in comparison with the works of earlier artists, is striking: above all it lacks the direct touch of the artist, whose contribution must certainly have been limited to the provision of a coloured sketch.

Zobi[52] quotes the following description of the piece made by Luigi Venturi, private secretary to the Grand Duke, at the time when it was first on view to the public:

'It is a circular table top, three Florentine yards in diameter, or 1·75 metres, with a background of the finest oriental lapis lazuli. In the centre is Apollo on his chariot decorated with the dance of the Hours, upheld by the clouds and drawn by four chargers. Apollo is restraining these so that he can descend among the nine muses. This subject has been made in imitation of a cameo in yellow Tuscan jasper, and must have been the most arduous part of the whole work because it reproduces the shading of a bas-relief. It has been done so finely, however, that the most diligent painter could not match it.

'This central subject is surrounded by a garland of two-coloured roses, which are an allusion to the dawn, interspersed with stars. The roses have been rendered by means of a red Guzzarate agate and the extremely rare golden-yellow Tuscan jasper which alters towards red; the stars are of Tuscan chalcedony. Round this part are nine almost circular partitions decorated with acanthus scrolls, and on each dividing section is a little lion's head. This sector is also of Tuscan jasper, while its chiaroscuro effect has been obtained by reference to the position of light which governs the whole work. Each of the nine partitions contains the symbols of the muse it intends to represent, and these have been made up from siliceous stones from all over the world.

'Following the established order, the first muse is Clio, who may be found beneath Apollo's chariot. The muse of history, she is represented here by papyrus and the laurel crown, as she was in the statues of the ancient Greeks and Romans. To the spectator's right is Euterpe, who represents music and whose symbols are two pipes tied together, again following the custom of antique monuments. Thalia, muse of comedy, has the cymbal and ivy crown, while Melpomene, muse of tragedy, has the tragic mask, that has been rendered so aptly by means of a rare flesh-coloured Tuscan chalcedony, and also the vine tendrils and grapes. Terpsichore, the muse of dance, has the ancient lyre, which has been copied from an original, and the laurel crown. The muse of lyrical and amorous poetry, Erato, has the lyre of Apollo. Polyhymnia, representing rhetoric or eloquence, has a crown of pink, red and violet roses, while Urania the astronomer, is given

99 Table top in commesso work, made in Prague. Vienna, Kunsthistorisches Museum.

her halo and globe adorned with the signs of the zodiac. Calliope, muse of heroic verse, has the wax tablets and the stylus which both writes and erases. Round these nine compartments encircling the central subject runs a large circular frieze displaying thirty-six clusters of flowers of all seasons, such as it is possible to represent in hard stone, in eighteen separate sections of two clusters each. Nine of these sections are placed in relation to the lion heads mentioned above, while the other nine are in relation to the nine compartments of the muses. The whole design is circumscribed by a border decorated with one hundred and thirty-five identical bosses in Tuscan chalcedony, each of which is enclosed in a fillet of the same stone; this border thus forms an elegant terminal to the work.'

This writer further comments that 'fourteen years were required to realise the design of the above-mentioned Giovanni Battista Giorgi and, thanks to the royal munificence, the diligence of the director of the Establishment, Cavaliere Carlo Siries, and the persevering cooperation of the craftsmen, every difficulty was overcome'.

This description gives a good idea of how carefully and how long men were able to work in that happy time upon projects of great costliness, so that exactly the right materials might be employed to interpret the design. The very meticulousness of the writer's description shows how closely mythology was studied to achieve this spectacular piece. Nowadays such labour would be considered out of the question, and the whole concept would be impossible. Later on, the author speaks of a cost of 'more than one hundred scudi', a truly fantastic figure. The support was modelled by Giovanni Dupré, and is also finely decorated with allegories. The minute attention to detail confirms the decadence of the art and the triumph of the craft. In fact this activity had already achieved its apogee, and required no further refinement. Yet one must indeed appreciate how accurately the material was chosen to obtain the desired effect, and how research into colour demanded the employment of rare stones which must have been extremely difficult to find.

Such refined work required the manufacture of special tools to cut the material, and the use of special supports to hold the tiny elements of the *commesso* which could hardly be held by fingers; and a suitable bed of adhesive resin and wax, strong enough to hold the pieces in place together during the lengthy processes of polishing, had to be found. To obtain suitable abrasives, siliceous sand was passed through a series of terracotta receptacles in a kind of cascade, so that the finest grains fell through while the coarser ones were trapped; in this way various grades of abrasive were collected. The Opificio was very thoroughly equipped, and was probably quite wealthy in view of the demand for its work.

Of the interminable series of works of this kind there remains a quantity of round, square and rectangular tables of the strangest design, among them are a view of the Baths at Montecatini, a view of the Villa delle Cascine and various porphyry pieces with designs of musical instruments and flowers. The designers and makers of these were Giorgi and Carlieri Carlo. These pieces were used as gifts between the reigning families of the time,[53] and it is recorded that one panel was sent to Francesco I, King of the two Sicilies, and another to Louis-Philippe, King of France, in 1843.

Work continued also on the Medici Chapel – work that had begun two centuries before and which is not yet finished today. The most impressive part is the altar, which had origi-

100 *View of Prague made of hard stones. Vienna, Kunsthistorisches Museum.*

101 *Shrine made of rock crystal and gold, with a background of* commesso *work. Vienna, Kunsthistorisches Museum.*

nally been projected by Matteo Nigetti and was too involved to be undertaken immediately. It was supposed to be decorated in a particular manner and in about 1824 Carlo Siries made Giovan Battista Giorgi produce designs of naturalistic and brightly-coloured decorations which were ill-suited to the formal parts which had already been executed, under the direction of Ferdinando I. Taste had changed, and the ruling neo-classicism overburdened with ornamentation clashed badly with the style of the earlier period. Wooden models were made that are still in existence, and panels of hard stone were applied to them to increase their effect. They are marvellous works of skill and concentrated effort, but they remain out of sympathy with the rest of the Chapel (Plate 93).

In 1838 a bronze foundry for reproducing antique sculpture was introduced into the Opificio which rather altered its character; then, as the fascination for new techniques developed, a workshop for galvanoplasty was added. From *commesso* works, enthusiasm passed to three dimensional pieces and gem cutting developed considerably. This led to the construction of the most complicated pedal-operated machinery, which this period of dreams and poetry saw fit to decorate with complex relief sculpture. The very workbench had become a work of art of solid walnut, decorated with cast bronze and furnished with a series of cases for tools and materials; sitting at this fine piece of furniture the artists must certainly have felt at their ease (Plate 64).

The Opificio[54] survived through still other political changes, as the war of independence developed. It saw the epoch of Garibaldi, the triumph of Victor Emanuel II, and the flight of the Grand Duke of Tuscany, Leopoldo, on 27 April 1859. It continued through all this quietly to design *commesso* flowers and butterflies as it had under the bland government of Ferdinando III, while busts of the Grand Duke, knocked down by the people in the streets, were given refuge in the storehouses of the institute, where they stayed until it was time for them to take their places in the museum. Now thoroughly used to political upheaval, the Opificio saw the crest of Lorraine above the doorway exchanged for the shield of Savoy, and the institute became an efficient branch of the Italian State. From 1865 to 1871 it was directed by Paolo Feroni. He was succeeded by Edoardo Marchionni, under whose guidance much work was completed in the long period until 1923. Much of his work is to be seen in the museum: it is naturalistic, precise and often of extraordinary effect (Plates 94, 95). There are pieces showing vases of flowers, animals and multi-coloured butterflies. The scenery of Zocchi's time was no longer in favour: now the subjects were methodical and pleasantly decorative.

Recent directors have paid much attention to restoration. The Opificio is now an autonomous institute of the Ministry of Public Instruction, maintained by the Department of Antiquities and Fine Arts. Study and research account for much of its activity, and there is still much work of restoration of mosaics, *intarsio*, gold-set gems and glazed terracotta, which is carried out throughout Italy and abroad. The workers and directors pride themselves upon their possession of the spirit of Francis I's 'Florentine Craftsmen' and continually refine their craft by the application of modern methods and criteria, thereby continuing the traditions that centuries have built up at this glorious institution.[55] But in Florence and elsewhere, other studios have sprung up which have become the modern centres of the same art.

102 *Table top in* commesso *work of hard stones and marble. London, British Museum.*

The family connections of the Medici[56] led Florentine artists also to Spain, where they produced fine work which resembles the Florentine both in technique and material (Plates 96, 97), examples of which are to be seen in the Prado Museum. Others, as has been described, went to France, while in seventeenth-century Prague there was a school of *commesso* in the Imperial workshops, found by two Florentines: Cosimo and Giovanni Castrucci[57] (Plates 98, 99, 100, 101). *Commesso* tables are also to be found in London at the British Museum (Plate 102). The name of Florence has indeed passed round the world and confirms today its centuries-old connection with art.

GLOSSARY

Agate From the Egyptian *hai*, 'to shine'. A variety of quartz, generally banded with concentric circles of various colours. All the names of precious stones are derived from roots meaning 'to shine', 'to burn'.

Bow file A tool adopted by mosaicists to hold a wire which is used for cutting the *commessi*, or inlays. It consists of a bow of chestnut wood or steel, and an iron wire or other soft metal, moistened with emery and water. The emery embeds itself in the metal in such a way that it can incise and cut hard materials.

Carborundum See *emery*.

Cassa The engraving effected in a material (wood, stone, marble) after a design layed down in advance and into which a decorative element is introduced, which constitutes the *intarsio*.

Cement Used in various senses in conjunction with the process of cementing (joining with cement). The latin *coementum* implies a kind of concrete made up of mortar and stone. Later, with the introduction of 'cement' in the sense of a hydraulic fixative towards the latter half of the last century, the word came to be used to designate various other adhesives used to bind together different materials such as mosaic *tesserae*. In these the adhesive frequently shows between the tiles where they do not meet precisely. Nowadays the word 'cement' is also used for the impasto base in which the tiles are laid, even though this may be made from lime.

Ceramics Used to describe all the products manufactured from clay, and these may be divided into two categories:

Porous, non-refractory terracotta, common brick, and refractory fire-clay products, maiolica ware (painted and glazed).

Stoneware and opaque pastes; translucent porcelain of vitreous structure. Ceramic *tesserae* are sometimes found in mosaic work, especially in oriental pieces.

Chalcedony Siliceous hard stone which takes its name from the ancient city of Chalcedon, in Asia Minor. It is a modification of microcystalline quartz and has a very compact structure: rayed, transparent and fibrous.

Chisel Cutting tool made of steel and consisting of a quadrangular section fixed into a wooden handle. It is used to break the *tesserae*.

Clay Clays are hydrated silicates of aluminium in the composition of which are found other silicates, ferric oxides, alkalis, calcium sulphates and organic material. They contain a certain quantity of water, and so may be plastic at the time of extraction from the beds. If quickly moulded they may be dried and hardened and retain their natural colours. Some primitive mosaic *tesserae* and conical tiles were made from clay. Their consistency is poor, however, and they deteriorate easily.

Coccio Literally a 'crock', and used in certain regions of Italy to mean a vase or ornamental piece of terracotta.

Cocciopesto A word derived from:
coccio, a piece in terracotta (*q.v.*).
pesto, a root of the verb *pestare*, to pound, to break into tiny fragments.

GLOSSARY

NOTES

BIBLIOGRAPHY

INDEX

Cocciopesto was used as an inert material which, when mixed with lime gave a pinkish colour to it. The resulting material was used either directly as a pavement by immediate application, or as a foundation in which mosaic *tesserae* were set to make a mosaic pavement.

Collante A material serving as an adhesive.

Commesso A type of 'sectional mosaic' which may be executed in marbles, hard or soft stones. It is called this because the individual pieces are so closely fitted together that the seams do not show. The pieces are then said to be '*commessi*', or combined. From the Latin *committere* 'to join together'.

Crustae Marble or other lapidary segments arranged following the outline of a design so as to give a figural composition (*opera sectilia*).

Drill A hole-forming tool consisting of a rotating element, the movement of which is continuous or alternating, and which is turned by hand, pedal or electricity. Percussion drills exist which operate at various speeds up to the ultrasonic. For boring hard stone (*q.v.*) ordinary points are not satisfactory: instead a metal tube of iron, brass or steel moistened with emery and water is employed. The emery encrusts the metal and cuts through the stone. The tubes are known as 'pipes'.

Emery An abrasive formed from granulated corundum mixed with ferric oxide. It is found commercially as a powder obtained by grinding materials extracted from mineral beds (Canada and Asia Minor). It is now more usually a substitute carborundum formed from a combination of carbon and silicates. Emery is employed as a cleaning agent upon the surface of mosaic work in hard stone, for which purpose it may be obtained in various grades of fineness. It is also used for cutting hard stone.

Foundation The surface prepared to receive mosaic paving. In antiquity it was usually composed of lime and sand, or volcanic or brick dust.

Gem Cutting The art of working hard stones, ivory, coral, etc., in three dimensions. The Italian word *glittica* or *gliptica* for this process comes from the Greek *glyptos*, a 'cut' or 'incision'. It is done with a saw (*q.v.*).

Grinding This is the first stage of polishing the surface of the mosaic and is done with emery or siliceous sand.

Grinding Wheel A wheel of varying thickness and diameter, turning upon a fixed or free axle, which grinds away various materials to make channels or cuts. It may be entirely made of a paste containing emery, or may be of metal, with only the external part (known as the crown) of abrasive material (emery, or, better still, diamond dust). It is often used in mosaic work and in *commessi* in hard stone where the tolerance between the different pieces must be very small.

Gum Mastic The word is probably derived from the name of a natural resin produced by the Lentiscus, which is cultivated in the tropics. It now usually implies a mixture of various substances to be prepared hot or cold, and is employed to fix the elements of a mosaic to a support. In antiquity the hot kind was prepared with resin mixed with other substances to delay hardening and make it less fragile.

Hard Stone Stone or mineral material with a hardness superior to the sixth degree in the Mohs scale of hardness.

Intarsio An inlay executed in various materials, some of which are embedded into the surface, and subsequently planed and polished to give a uniform surface on a single plane. *Intarsio* differs from *tarsio* work in that the entire surface is not covered.

Jasper A variety of microcrystalline quartz which is very compact, opaque, and which may be variegated.

Lime Material obtained by high-temperature firing of the more or less pure limestones in special kilns. Immediately after it has been taken from the kilns it is known as quicklime. When moistened with water it swells and hydrates, giving out much heat, and eventually becomes a powder. More water may then be added so as to obtain 'slaked lime'. Mixed with sand, it becomes extremely hard as a result of carbonisation and is very long-lasting. The impasto thus obtained can be used as the chip or plaster foundation on which the *tesserae* are placed.

Lithostroton A Greek word formed from *lithos*, 'a stone', and *stroo*, 'a pavement'; not necessarily a mosaic pavement.

Mason's Hammer A small steel hammer with two cutting edges on the head. It is used for cutting the materials for mosaic tiles, in contrast with the chisel (*q.v.*).

Mother-of-Pearl The shining and iridescent internal surface of many shells especially of the pearl-giving oyster. It is composed of very thin layers of calcium carbonate together with conchiferous material. It is used in mosaic and especially in *commesso* work to give particular effects, although it is not particularly hard and chips easily.

Onyx A word derived from:
The Greek *onyx*, 'a fingernail', since colouration is often similar to that of a fingernail.
The coptic *uoein*, 'to shine'. A transparent variety of quartz which may be polished.

Opificio From the Latin *opificium* or *opifex* 'artificer', 'maker', 'craftsman'. It means office, laboratory or workshop.

Opus A Latin word meaning 'life-work' or work in general.

Opus alexandrinum A type of mosaic executed with small lapidary elements of quadrangular shape, and generally in black and white disposed in a pattern upon a background surface almost invariably pinkish in colour.

Opus sectile A type of mosaic work in which *tesserae* are not used for the figures of a design, but instead pieces of marble or other stones are specially cut so as to form either uniformly coloured or variously toned areas, according to the material employed.

Opus segmentatum A pavement made by inserting chips or coarse lapidary segments into the mortar. The term, which is widely used by archeologists, is considered inaccurate by some authorities (see G. Becatti, *op. cit.*, p. 254).

Opus signinum The Roman name for a very simple kind of pavement mosaic made from river gravels, or a mixture of small stone pieces, lime or *cocciopesto*, which lends the whole a pinkish colour. With this work, the finer the gravel and the impasto, the more pleasing the result.

Opus tasselatum or tesselatum A more involved version of *opus alexandrinum* made from lapidary elements or coloured vitreous paste, cut in practically uniform quadrangular sections but having variable thicknesses and so tightly packed as to render the background invisible. The name derives from the elements of the work – the *tesserae* or *tesselae*.

Opus vermiculatum A more refined and more costly type of mosaic than those mentioned above, in which the artist varies the shape of the tesserae so that they sometimes assume curious patterns which resemble '*vermi*' or worms.

Pavimentum barbaricum A very simple, rough kind of paving, generally beaten into some kind of impasto.

Pebble A stone rounded by river flow and often ovoidal. Examples in jasper, generally lined or banded, were collected from the river Arno at Florence or elsewhere in Tuscany from the period of the Medicis, and were sliced and then used in mosaic work.

Pipe See *Drill*.

Polishing The second stage of work required to give a shine to the surface of a mosaic. It is done by means of very fine abrasives.

Pozzolana A variety of volcanic tufa of poor consistency which is formed by the disintegration of lava slag. When reduced to a powder and mixed with lime it has adhesive qualities even under water. It was much employed in ancient Rome, and even today it is in general use in Lazio and the Roman Campania as a wall-stucco. It is found in the neighbourhood of Naples, and in the Islands of Lipari and Santorini in the Aegean.

Pumice-Stone A vitreous volcanic rock known in geology as obsidian. Obsidian is generally black in colour, and has a high silica content. Where the structure is porous the colour is lighter, and it may be called pumice or obsidian; in this state it is light enough to float in water. Heated to a high temperature, obsidian may become pumice. It then serves as a light abrasive for work on the surface of a mosaic or on inlays of marble or hard stone. It may be used either in a piece or as a powder.

Rocks Aggregates of various materials, usually of considerable size, geologically identifiable, and forming the so-called earth's crust.

Rotino A grinding wheel of very small size. Since it runs on a free axle it may be operated manually.

Sand A mass of tiny particles of stone and other minerals produced generally by sea or river action. According to its provenance it may contain siliceous, micaceous, calcareous and other materials, and even precious minerals. It is classified according to its composition and the purity of the grains. It is found in rivers, on seabeds and in caves. It is generally made up into an impasto with lime, whereupon it is known as mortar, or *rena* in some Italian dialects. A siliceous type is used as an abrasive which is effective also upon hard stone.

Saw Tool for cutting, or, as mosaicists call it, slicing the stone. It consists of a narrow blade of iron oscillating horizontally in opposing directions. It invariably moves over a vertical plane, progressing downwards within this plane. It is whetted with siliceous sand or emery and water as is the bow-saw wire. The blade becomes encrusted with emery, the obtrusive points of which cut the material.

Shales and Slates These are clay schists easily divisible into sheets. They are selected for fine grain and for the degree of ease with which they may be sliced. Slate is found in many parts of Liguria and is used in sheets as a foundation for *commesso* work or for portable mosaics.

Shining up The last stage in work on the surface of the mosaic and must be undertaken with the greatest care. The work should take place in a dust-free environment where emery is not used. Shining up requires much time, patience, and the use of metal oxides reduced to the finest powder and mixed with water. The abrasive is worked with wood blocks, paper, or canvas.

Slice A piece of hard stone having two parallel facets. Such a slice is usually very thin, perhaps a few millimetres in depth; this varies according to breadth and other considerations. The slices are obtained by means of a saw (*q.v.*).

Smalto (Enamel)
1 A vitreous coloured layer supported on various materials, but in the case of mosaic work almost always on terracotta or porcelain. It serves for use as *tesserae* where vitreous pastes are not used. Such enamels are obtained by fusion within special kilns after the carrying surface has been covered with a thin layer of a metal oxide which will vary according to the colour desired.
2 Composed of gravels, sand and slaked lime; made up into an impasto with water, it too serves as a foundation to which mosaic paving may be applied.

Soft Stone Stone or mineral material with a hardness inferior to the 6th degree of the Mohs scale of hardness.

Sottosquadra Under-squaring: a particular way of cutting the pieces of a *commesso* so that they do not present a right angle in respect of the plane in which the whole lies. Hence '*non a squadra*' (not at right angles) describes what is not at ninety degrees – not square, but at an acute angle that may allow it to be fitted into its place more easily. Naturally the acute angle occurs on the upper surface.

Spatula A tool used for applying gum mastics and other adhesives. It is made of wood or iron. Its central part is rounded, while the extremities may be flattened into various shapes.

Support Used to carry the pieces that compose the portable mosaic, *commesso* or inlay.

Tarsio Inlay: a design or figure composed of many tiny elements cut according to a pattern, and attached to a support.

Terracotta A clay which has been brought to a high temperature in a kiln and become baked, hardened and coloured, and so strengthened. Clays used for this purpose contain certain ferruginous, calcareous and siliceous impurities which impart varying degrees of colour to the terracotta, usually yellows and reds.

Tesserae Fragments of marble, stone, terracotta, glass, enamelled and other materials which are used to make up certain types of mosaic. Generally cubical in form, they vary in size within the range of a few centimetres.

Turning-lathe This is one of the most ancient pieces of machinery, and is used almost invariably rotating horizontally to produce turned surfaces and occasionally flat surfaces.

Variegated Showing differences of colour such as may be encountered in the surface of a marble or hard stone, and which result from the presence or addition of various elements in the mass of the material.

Vitreous Paste Variously coloured materials made of fused glass, and from which tesserae may be obtained. For practical purposes, such tesserae almost always have a thickness of about one centimetre.

NOTES

I. MOSAICS

1. Pliny, *Naturalis Historiae*, XXXVI, 61.
2. *Enciclopedia Italiana*, section on mosaics, p. 77, Rome, 1934.
3. Furio Fasolo and Giorgio Gullini, *Il santuario della Fortuna Primigenia a Palestrina*, p. 312, Rome, 1953. The interpretation that Gullini places upon Pliny's words is not accepted by everyone: *see* Becatti, *Scavi di Ostia*, p. 254.
4. Pliny, *op. cit.*, XXXVI, 184.
5. *Enciclopedia Italiana* (mosaics), p. 78.
6. Pericle Ducati, *L'Arte Classica*, p. 53, Turin, 1939.
7. G. B. Milani and F. Fasolo, *Le Forme Architettoniche*, vol. I, p. 80, Milan, 1931.
8. Tea Eva, *Preistoria Civiltà Extraeuropee*, p. 230, Turin, 1953.
9. Mia Cinotti, *Arte di tutti i tempi*, p. 49, Novara, 1955.
10. Pliny, *op. cit.*, XXXVI, 26, 65.
11. *Enciclopedia dell' Arte antica classica e orientale*, p. 228, Rome, 1958.
12. *Ibid*.
13. Mario Bussagli, note in *Enciclopedia Universale dell' Arte*, vol. IX, p. 597, Florence, 1963.
14. S. Dimand, *Enciclopedia Universale dell' Arte*, vol. IX, p. 696 ff.
15. S. Dimand, *op. cit.*
16. Herman Goetz, *Enciclopedia Universale dell' Arte*, *op. cit.*, vol. IX, p. 698.
17. E. Lavagnino, *L'Arte medioevale*, p. 14, Turin, 1953.
18. Pericle Ducati, *L'Arte Classica*, p. 532, Turin, 1939.
19. G. E. Rizzo, *La pittura ellenistico-romana*, p. 29 ff, Milan, 1929.
20. Giorgio Gullini, *I mosaici di Palestrina*, p. 18, Rome, 1956.
21. V. Gerspach, *La mosaïque*, pp. 26–30, Paris, 1878.
22. P. Ducati, *op. cit.*, p. 533.
23. G. E. Rizzo, *op. cit.*, p. 80 ff.
24. F. Fasolo and G. Gullini, *op. cit.*, p. 312 ff.
25. G. Gullini, *op. cit.*
26. G. Gullini, *op. cit.*, p. 33.
27. G. Gullini, *op. cit.*, p. 48.
28. Giovanni Becatti, *Scavi di Ostia*, vol. IV, 'Mosaici e pavimenti marmorei', p. 248 ff, Istituto poligrafico dello Stato, Rome, 1961.
29. M. van Berchen and E. Clouzot, *Mosaïques chrétiennes du IV au X siècles*, Geneva, 1924.
30. Vasile Canarache, *Muzuel de archeologie din Coustanta*, pp. 81, 82, Bucharest, 1967; study and restoration of this pavement are currently being undertaken by Professor Richard Bordenache, Director of the Historical Monuments Department of Rumania.
31. E. Kitzinger, *Enciclopedia Universale dell' Arte, op. cit.*, vol. IX.
32. Pietro Toesca, *Storia dell' Arte Italiana*, note 56, p. 78, Turin, 1914.
33. E. Lavagnino, *op. cit.*, p. 65.
34. Adolfo Venturi, *Mosaici cristiani in Roma*, p. 7, Florence, 1958.
35. P. Ducati, *op. cit.*, p. 716.
36. G. Bovini, *Mosaici di Ravenna*, p. 27, Milan, 1956.
37. E. Lavagnino, *op. cit.*, p. 119.
38. P. Toesca and F. Forlati, *Mosaici di San Marco*, Milan, 1957.
39. P. Toesca and F. Forlati, *op. cit.*
40. E. Lavagnino, *op. cit.*, p. 384.
41. P. Toesca and F. Forlati, *op. cit.*, p. 8.
42. P. Toesca and F. Forlati, *op. cit.*, p. 11.
43. A. de Witt, *I mosaici del Battistero di Firenze*, Florence, 1954.
44. W. and E. Soate, *Die Wirchen von Florenz*, Frankfurt, 1952–1955.

45 A. de Witt, *op. cit.*, vol. I.
46 A. de Witt, *op. cit.*, vol. III.
47 See also Chapter IV of the present work.
48 A. de Witt, *op. cit.*, vol. III.
49 G. Trenta, *I mosaici del duomo di Pisa e i loro autori*, Florence, 1896.
50 Guglielmo Matthiae, *Mosaici medioevali delle chiese di Roma*, p. 69, Rome, 1967.
51 E. Lavagnino, *op. cit.*, p. 68.
52 G. Matthiae, *op. cit.*, p. 69 ff.
53 G. Matthiae, *op. cit.*, p. 379.
54 G. Matthiae, *op. cit.*, p. 120.
55 E. Lavagnino, *op. cit.*, p. 72.
56 V. Gerspach, *op. cit.*, p. 152.
57 E. Lavagnino, *op. cit.*, p. 406.
58 Pietro Cavallini: Roman painter and innovator who worked at the end of the thirteenth and beginning of the fourteenth centuries.
59 G. Matthiae, *op. cit.*, p. 374.
60 E. Lavagnino, *op. cit.*, p. 400.
61 E. Lavagnino, *op. cit.*, p. 404.
62 V. Gerspach, *op. cit.*, p. 158.
63 V. Gerspach, *op. cit.*, p. 164.
64 E. Lavagnino, *op. cit.*, p. 373 ff.
65 E. Lavagnino, *op. cit.*, p. 376.
66 E. Lavagnino, *op. cit.*, p. 380.
67 E. Lavagnino, *op. cit.*, p. 381.
68 V. Gerspach, *La Mosaïque*, Paris, 1878.
69 E. Kitzinger, *op. cit.*
70 E. Kitzinger, *op. cit.*
71 E. Kitzinger, *op. cit.*
72 E. Kitzinger, *op. cit.*
73 Mons. Grazio Gianfreda, *Il mosaico pavimentale della basilica cattedrale di Otranto*, Alassio di Casamari (Frosinone), 1965.
74 V. Gerspach, *op. cit.*, p. 121.
75 V. Gerspach, *op. cit.*, p. 186 ff.
76 V. Gerspach, *op. cit.*, p. 228.
77 E. Kitzinger, *op. cit.*
78 E. Lavagnino, *op. cit.*, pp. 267, 268.

II. INTARSIO WORK

1 Michelangelo Cagiano di Azevedo; note in *Enciclopedia Universale dell' Arte*, vol. VII, Florence, 1958.
2 Pliny, *op. cit.*, XXXVI.
3 Pliny, *op. cit.*, 61.

4 *Enciclopedia Italiana*, p. 77, Rome, 1934.
5 Gustave Soulier, *Les influences orientales dans la peinture toscane*, p. 37, Paris, 1924.
6 G. Soulier, *op. cit.*, p. 45.
7 E. Lavagnino, *op. cit.*, p. 496.
8 E. Lavagnino, *op. cit.*, p. 334 ff.
9 Nicolò Pericoli, known as 'il Tribolo', sculptor and architect, Florence (1500–1558).
10 André Chastel, *Enciclopedia universale dell' Arte*, Florence, 1958.
11 Vincenzo Golzio, *Il Seicento e il Settecento*, Turin, 1950.
12 Giacomo Barozzi da Vignola (Modena), architect and writer (1507–1573).
13 H. Goetz, note in *Enciclopedia dell' Arte*, vol. IX, p. 698.
14 *Forma e Colore*, no. 52, Florence, 1967.

IV. COMMESSO WORK

1 A. Zobi, *Notizie storiche nell' origine e progressi di lavori in commesso in pietre dure*, p. 29, Florence, 1853.
2 R. Brauns, *Il regno minerale*, p. 278, Milan, 1906.
3 A. Zobi, *op. cit.*, p. 190 ff.
4 F. Baldinucci (Florence, 1624–1696), *Delle notizie de' professori del disegno*, Florence, 1771.
5 Ferdinando Rossi, *Gioielli e pietre dure alla Corte Medicea*, Florence, 1966, 'Notiziario Antichita e Belle Arti', nos. 24, 25.
6 A. Zobi, *op. cit.*, pp. 48, 49.
7 A. Morassi, *Il tesoro dei Medici*, Milan, 1963.
8 A. Zobi, *op. cit.*, pp. 48, 49.
9 A. Morassi, *op. cit.*, p. 1.
10 G. F. Young, *I Medici*, vol. I, p. 202, Florence, 1949.
11 G. F. Young, *op. cit.*, p. 212.
12 A. Zobi, *op. cit.*, p. 76.
13 A. Morassi, *op. cit.*, p. 27.
14 A. Zobi, *op. cit.*, p. 199.
15 A. Zobi, *op. cit.*, pp. 183, 184.
16 A. Zobi, *op. cit.*, p. 153.
17 A. Zobi, *op. cit.*, p. 162.
18 Bernardo Buontalenti (1536–1608): he learned much from Michelangelo Buonarroti and Giorgio Vasari and was one of the most significant architects of the late Renaissance, continuing the tradition of research that humanism developed.

He was closely connected with the Medici, and helped the Grand Duke Francis in his experiments with fireworks. His nickname 'Bernardo delle girandole' was given for this latter work, and many believe that he was the inventor of the catherine wheel. He was a director of the Opificio delle Pietre Dure, and did much work on the project for the Medici chapel in San Lorenzo.

He was also a goldsmith, and some of his vases in lapis lazuli and gold are preserved in the Museo degli Argenti in Florence. According to Zobi, Bernardo Buontalenti in 1601 had already designed the ciborium in hard stone which was destined for the great Chapel, and the whole gallery was at work on this piece which was to be so magnificent; however, even before, in 1599, 'Tommaso di Fabiano, Marcutt di Marcutt and Cristoforo Paurr had begun a model in full size'.

19 Matteo Nigetti: born probably in Florence between 1560 and 1570. Like his father, he began by working in wood, but learnt sculpture and so was able to make restorations in the Grand Duke's Gallery. A student of Buontalenti, he learnt architecture and did much work on the construction of the Chapel of San Lorenzo. Zobi names him as a director of the Opificio delle Pietre Dure. Various other architectural works in Florence are his, as is the chapel of the Virgin in the Church of San Nicola in Pisa.

20 Ludovico Cardi, known also as 'Cigoli', (1559–1613): Closely connected with the Medici, he was unable to escape their passion for ornamental stonework which led, towards the end of the sixteenth century, to the construction of the chapel destined to be the family mausoleum.

21 In speaking of Bilivert, the name that leaps to mind is that of Giovanni, a painter and student of 'Cigoli' and an important man at the Medici Court; yet his brother Giacomo was also of importance there, and was one of those who took part in the battles between Flemish and Florentine craftsmen during the period.

22 A. Zobi, *op. cit.*, p. 217.
23 A. Zobi, *op. cit.*, p. 167.
24 Francesco Settimanni, *Cronica Fiorentina inedita* (seventeenth century) in the Medici Archives, now State Archives.
25 From Luciano Berti, *see* Bibliography.
26 *Ibid.*
27 F. Baldinucci, *op. cit.*
28 A. Zobi, *op. cit.*, p. 199.
29 F. Baldinucci, *op. cit.*
30 A. Zobi, *op. cit.*, p. 231.
31 A. Zobi, *op. cit.*, p. 229 (on the subject of Constantino de' Servi).
32 A. Zobi, *op. cit.*, p. 235.
33 Celano, *ed.* Charini, vol. IV, pp. 587, 579, Naples.
34 *Napoli nobilissima*, IX, pp. 178, 9, 1900; *Napoli e luoghi celebri delle sue vicinanze*, Naples, 1845; Romanelli, *Napoli antica e moderna*, pp. 160, 161.
35 Celano, *op. cit.*
36 Giovanni Tescione, 'Il laboratorio delle pietre dure di Napoli e l'altare della cappella Palatina della reggia di Caserta'. From *Studi in onore di Riccardo Filangieri*, vol. III.
37 G. F. Young, *I Medici*, vol. II, p. 399, Florence, 1949.
38 Goa is in India on the coast of Malabar and is surrounded by the territory of Bombay.
39 A. Zobi, *op. cit.*, p. 249.
40 Mario Bussagli, *Forma e Colore*, no. 52, Florence, 1967. (The colour plates are reproduced by permission of Edizioni Sansoni.)
41 G. F. Young, *op. cit.*, vol. II, p. 373.
42 E. Petrasch, *Schloss Favorite*, Karlsruhe, 1960.
43 G. F. Young, *op. cit.*, vol. II, p. 409.
44 E. Petrasch, *op. cit.*
45 A. Zobi, *op. cit.*, p. 272.
46 G. F. Young, *op. cit.*, vol. II, p. 451.
47 Giuseppe Zocchi was born in Florence in 1711, and was educated by the Gerini family, who sent him to the great cultural centres of the day – Rome, Bologna, Milan and Venice. In the latter city, Zocchi fell under the influence of the Swiss painter Joseph Wagner and the Venetian school of painters of views and *capricci*. This formed his taste for landscape and city views. His work for the Opificio delle Pietre Dure is less well known; however, several of his canvases are preserved in the museum of the Opificio, some of which at least were made into *commesso*.
48 A. Zobi, *op. cit.*, p. 296.
49 L. Bartoli and E. Maser, *Il Museo delle Pietre Dure di Firenze*, p. 12, Florence, 1959.
50 A. Zobi, *op. cit.*, p. 347.
51 A. Zobi, *op. cit.*, p. 304.
52 A. Zobi, *op. cit.*, p. 307.
53 A. Zobi, *op. cit.*, p. 303.

54   A. Zobi, *op. cit.*, p. 326.
55   A list of all directors and workers of the Opificio from its foundation to the present (*see* A. Zobi, *op. cit.* p. 341 ff.)

During the reigns of Francesco I and Ferdinando I (21 April 1574 – 3 February 1609):

Directors: Cavalieri (De'), Emilio (Superintendant general); Latini, Cosimo (*Provveditore*); Buontalenti, Bernardo; Servi (De'), Costantino; Nigetti, Matteo.

Master craftsmen: Leccio (da), Porfirio di Bernardino; (Commesso work began during the reign of Cosimo I) Pastorini, Pastorino, of Siena; Caccini, Giulio, of Florence; Caccini, Michele, of Florence; Sinibaldi, Sinibaldo, of Florence; Landi, Niccolò, of Lucca; Buontalenti, Bernardo, painter, architect and sculptor; Bianchi, Giovanni, of Milan; Carroni, Giann' Ambrogio, of Milan; Carroni, Gian Stefano, of Milan; Gaffuri, Giorgio, of Milan; Gaffuri, Cristoforo, of Milan; Gaffuri, Bernardino, of Milan; Matre (de), Guglielmo, of France; Murval, Daniello, of France; Hiermann or Herman, Bartolommeo, of Germany; Marchesini, Giuseppe (ruby worker), of Venice; Bruni, Antonio, of Florence; Studendoli, Pompeo (diamond worker), of Venice; Ferrucci, Francesco, of Florence; Santini, Andrea, of Florence; Simoni, Urbano, of Florence; Davanzati, Alessandro, of Florence; Tasso (del), Domenico, of Florence; Palai, Michelangelo, of Florence; Flach, Giacomo, of Germany; Paoli, Pietro (goldsmith), of Florence; Santucci, Antonio (goldsmith), of Florence; Bartolommei, Agostino (goldsmith), of Florence.

Designers: Papi, Cristoforo (known as L'Altissimo), of Florence; Mariotti, Andrea (known as 'il Minga'), of Florence; Ligozzi, Jacopo (painter), of Verona; Marchetti, Bartolo (miniaturist), of Venice; Cardi, Ludovico (known as 'il Cigoli'), of Tuscany; Barbatelli, Bernardino (known as 'il Poccetti'), of Tuscany; Marucelli, Valerio, of Florence; Flosch, Daniello, of Belgium; Bologna, Giovanni (sculptor), of Douai.

During the reign of Cosimo II (3 February 1609 – 28 February 1621)

Directors: Balatri, Giovanni Battista (architect), of Florence; Tacca, Pietro (sculptor), of Carrara.

Master craftsmen: Ottaviani, Cammillo, of Florence; Albertini, Pietro, of Florence; Borgognoni, Andrea (portrait painter), of Florence; Gatti, Iacopo, of Florence; Cappelli, Baccio, senior, of Florence; Capelli, Giovanni, of Florence; Dame (Delle), Giovanni, of Florence; Cangi, Orazio, of Florence; Sassi, Giovanni Battista, of Florence; Hener, Cosimo, of Germany; Nelli, Vincenzo (goldsmith), of Florence; Falchi, Giona (goldsmith), of Florence; Domenichi, Cassiano (goldsmith), of Florence.

Designers: Bilivert, Giovanni (painter), of Florence; Mola, Gaspero (designer of coins and medals), of Rome.

During the reign of Ferdinando II (28 February 1621 – 23 May 1670)

Directors and Designers: Autelli, Jacopo (painter), of Florence; Bianco (Del), Baccio (engineer and painter), of Florence; Mochi, Orazio, of Florence; Mochi, Francesco d'Orazio, of Florence.

Master craftsmen: Comparini, Giovanni Francesco, of Florence; Pandolfini, Giuliano, of Florence; Martini, Anton Francesco, of Florence; Ghinghi, Andrea, of Florence; Sorbi, Antonio, of Florence; Alberighi, Angelo, of Florence; Vestri, Aurelio, of Florence; Cappelli, Antonio, of Florence; Hener, Antonio, of Germany; Winchler, Cristoforo, of Germany; Migliorini, Ferdinando, of Florence (later worked in France); Merlini, Giovanni, of Florence; Giachetti, Giovanni, of Florence; Cappelli, Baccio Junior, of Florence; Giorgi, Giovanni, of Florence; Bottini, Giovanni Francesco, of Florence; Bottini, Lorenzo, of Florence; Bianchi, Giovanni, of Florence; Centelli, Carlo, of Florence; Focardi, Sebastiano (flower worker), of Florence.

During the reign of Cosimo III (23 May 1670 – 31 October 1723)

Master craftsmen: Bamberini, Giuseppe, of Florence; Bizzarri, Giuseppe, of Florence; Brogelli, Giovanni, of Florence; Bianchi, Giovanni Domenico, of Florence; Volpi, Giuseppe, of Florence; Ramponi, Giuseppe, of Florence; Torricelli, Giuseppe, of Florence; Torricelli, Antonio, of Florence; Fanciullacci, Marco, of Florence; Montauti, Giovanni Battista, of Florence; Belli, Lorenzo, of Florence; Sorbi, Mattias, of Florence; Valori, Niccolò, of Florence; Giovannelli, Ottavio, of Florence; Zucconi, Giovanni Battista, of Florence; Muffati, Raffaello, of Florence; (Muffati and Zucconi later worked in Naples);

Borghesi, Pietro, of Florence; Poggi, Santi, of Florence; Volpi, Tommaso, of Florence.

Designers and Assistants: (Cosimo III suppressed the post of Director, passing its duties to the *guardaroba maggiore*, while the work of directing the *commessi* was given to the designer having the title of 'assistant'.) Scacciati, Michele (painter), of Florence; Ciaminghi, Francesco, of Florence.

During the reign of Gian Gastone (31 October 1723 – 9 July 1737)

Master craftsmen: Botti, Paolo, of Florence; Ciolli, Antonio, of Florence; Botti, Francesco Senior, of Florence; Cioni, Anton Francesco (portrait painter), of Florence; Burci, Benedetto (still-life painter), of Florence; Campi, Francesco, of Florence; Violi, Filippo, of Florence; Minchioni, Giuseppe, of Florence; (Campi, Violi and Minchioni later worked in Naples); Torricelli, Bartolommeo, of Florence; Botti, Carlo Francesco, of Florence; Pretolani, Matteo, of Florence; Formigli, Cosimo, of Florence; Migliorini, Ferdinando Junior, of Florence; Weber, Lorenzo (coin maker); Soldani, Massimiliano (bronze founder), of Florence; Siries, Louis (gem and cameo cutter), of France.

Assistants: Scacciati, Pietro di Michele (designer), of Florence. A list of the *Guardaroba Maggiori* (courtesy of the State Archives of Florence): Marchese Del Monte, Cerbone (1652–1688); Marchese Ferroni, Francesco (temporary, 1690–1693); Marchese Incontri, Attilio (9 April 1695 – 17 June 1713); Quaratesi, Antonino, General Superintendant of the Gallery 'pro Interni' succeeded Incontri from 19 June 1713 – 7 August 1713; Marchese Corsini, Bartolommeo (13 August 1713 – 13 February 1722); Marchese Riccardi, Cosimo (16 March 1722 – 13 May 1735); Marchese Riccardi, Vincenzo succeeded his father Cosimo from 13 May 1735–1752; Marchese Riccardi, Bernardino (26 April 1753–1766).

During the reign of Francesco II (Dynasty of Lorraine) (9 July 1737 – 17 August 1765)

Zobi remarks: 'In April 1749, Pietro Scacciati retired and the title of *Custode* and *Assistente* was suppressed, and that of *Ispettore* substituted, for which latter post Louis Siries was nominated. On 21 June 1759, Louis being old, he retired and his son Cosimo succeeded him, while Louis himself was given the title of *Direttore*, now reinstated.'

Master craftsmen: Torricelli, Gaetano, of Florence; Borghesi, Francesco, of Florence; Cappelli, Baccio Junior, of Florence; Babuini, Ignazio, of Florence; Botti, Anton Francesco, of Florence; Jacopucci, Gaspero, of Florence; Jacopucci, Francesco, of Florence.

Designers: Conti, Francesco (painter), of Florence; Zocchi, Giuseppe (painter), of Florence.

During the reign of Leopoldo I (18 August 1765 – 7 March 1791)

Directors: Cosimo Siries until 1789, when he was succeeded upon his death by his son Louis Junior.

Master craftsmen: Mosti, Pietro, of Florence; Minossi, Gaspero, of Florence; Dini, Benedetto, of Florence; Bernabé, Felice (cutter).

Designers and Selectors of stones: Cioci, Antonio, of Florence.

Storekeeper: Giusti, Pietro, of Florence.

During the reign of Ferdinando III (7 March 1791 – 18 June 1824)

Directors: Louis Siries, upon whose death his son Carlo succeeded to the post by decree of the Emperor Napoleon (1812).

Master craftsmen: (serving under the Napoleonic and Bourbon domination) Scheggi, Giovanni, of Florence; Merciai, Antonio, of Florence; Buoninsegni, Luigi, of Florence; Ragionieri, Francesco, of Florence.

Designers and Selectors of stones: Cioci, Leopoldo, of Florence; Carlieri, Carlo, of Florence; Giorgi, Giovanni Battista, of Florence.

Storekeepers: Jacopucci, Damiano, of Florence; Tani, Sigismondo of Florence.

During the reign of Leopoldo II (18 June 1824 – December 1859)

Directors: Carlo Siries, succeeded upon his death in 1854 by the Secretary Alessandro Landi who retired in 1860, and whose duties were undertaken by Niccolò Betti until a new director was appointed.

Master craftsmen: Barbensi, Pietro; Merlini, Giuseppe; Pucci, Giovanni; Buoninsegni, Giuseppe; Manzini, Tito; Barbensi, Gelasio; Galli, Enrico; Merlini, Damiano; Merlini, Niccolò; Ragionieri, Francesco; (steward), Landi, Giuseppe; Renai, Pietro; Cioci, Francesco; Jacopucci, Damiano; Nannuncci, Giuseppe (bronze-caster and storekeeper), Gabbrielli, Giovanni; Bianchi, Angiolo; Giovannoni, Giovanni; Renai, Angiolo; Pucci, Alessandro;

Ninni, Anastasio; Barontini, Ferdinando; Gambacorta, Ferdinando (economic secretary); Pigli, Pietro; Del Fine, Alessandro (master bronze-caster); Bensi, Pietro (bronze-caster); Ugolini, Giovanni; Pucci, Tito; Igundetti, Jacopo; Galli, Enrico (economic secretary); Cadecasa, Raffaello; Pietro, Bargioni; Raffaello, Lessi; Piazzini, Cesare.

Designers and Selectors of stones: Giorgi, Giovanni; Battista and Betti Niccola.

Inspectors: Poggi, Giovanni; Merciai, Antonio.

Doorkeepers: Fantaccini, Pietro; Biondi, Francesco; Fiani, Pietro; Del Polla, Niccolò; Facetti, Ferdinando; Enrico, Hurault.

During the reign of Victor Emmanuel II (1860–1878)

In 1860, the reorganisation of the Uffici after the new administrative order of the Italian State led once more to the suppression of the post of director of the Real Officina delle Pietre Dure, while its duties now became the responsibility of the Director of Museums in Florence, Paolo Feroni.

At the same time, Niccolò Betti discharged the duties of Director of the Opificio delle Pietre Dure until 1873. In 1868 Eduardo Marchionni was nominated vice-director, and in 1876, director.

Master craftsmen: Paolo Ricci (work in relief and chief of office); Battistoni, Francesco (cutter); Turchini, Raffaello (mechanic); Angelo, Chiti; Emilio, Celati; Mattolini, Adolfo (assistant worker in relief); Brunacci, Pietro Fiesolano (master of the sawsmen); Cecchi, Ferdinando; Castellani, David; Grazzini, Gino; Nannucci, Cesare; Bichi, Giovanni (sawsman); Marucelli, Luigi; Belloni, Bernardo (sawsman); Dei, David; Merlini, Oreste; Betti, Enrico; Falli, Francesco; Balleggi, Gaetano (sawsman); Dei, Francesco; Gherardi, Goffredo; Damiani, Emilio; Castellani, Cesare; Gambacorti, Ferdinando (economic adviser); Franchini, Angelo (master of the sawsmen); Buyet, Stanislao (mechanic).

Designer and Selector of stones: Tito Giorgi.

Inspectors: Cavaliere Antonino Pepi, Galletti, Augusto (secretary).

Custodians: Gabriello Romolini, Ferdinando Martelli, Meini, Benedetto; Della Bella, Pasquale.

During the reign of Umberto I (1878–1900)

Director: Edoardo Marchionni.

Master craftsmen: Reggioli, Antonio; Barinci, Torello (tesserae mosaicist); Tortoli, Dionisio (sawsman); Merlini, Aretafilo (chief of laboratory); Mattolini, Adolfo (relief work and chief of laboratory); Renai, Ettore (chief of laboratory); Galardini, Pasquale; Casini, Tito.

Designer and Selector of stones: Massai, Ludovico (vice director and assistant chief of laboratory).

Inspectors: Cavaliere Antonino Pepi, Carnecchia, Emilio; Ferrari, Francesco.

Accountants: Gori, Giulio; Neri, Ermanno.

Custodians: Capecchi, Carlo; Gironda, Francesco.

During the reign of Victor Emmanuel III (1900–1945)

Directors: Edoardo Marchionni until his death in 1923. Alessandro Cerrina Feroni thereupon filled the post temporarily, until Amedeo Orlandini was nominated director in 1927.

Master craftsmen: Alessandro Cerrina Feroni (trustee and economic secretary); Galardini, Pasquale; Mattolini, Adolfo (work in relief); Camiciottoli, Panfilio; Michetti, Tito; Nencioni, Enrico; Casini, Tito; Capecchi, Piero; Pratesi, Guido; Renai, Ettore (chief of works); Conti, Orazio; Mannucci, Guido; Freni, Antonio; Neri, Cesare; Massai, Enrico; Bettaccini, Lorenzo; Bichi, Italo; Gabbrielli, Giovanni; Vaggelli, Raffaello; Cianferoni, Giuseppe; Toti, Vittorio; Biliotti, Azelio; Nannucci, Pilade (mosaicist); Marinai, Torquato (mosaicist); Bini, Marcello; Ciampi, Renzo; Ghizzoni, Guido; Bresci, Renato; Andorlini, Rodolfo (mosaicist); Baldi, Tebaldo; Bramanti, Vittorio; Mecocci, Alessandro; Viciani, Giuliano.

Technical Chief: Del Sarto, Angelo.

Technical Assistants: Ragionieri, Carlo; Santoni, Augusto; Biliotti, Alfonso.

Custodians: Capecchi, Carlo; Gironda, Francesco; Casebasse, Renato; Scheggi, Antonio; Barucchiere, Vincenzo; Nistri, Adone; Bini, Carlo; Fantoni, Bruno.

During the Italian Republic

Directors: Amedeo Orlandini, Professor of Architecture 1946–1949; Lando Bartoli, architect, 1950–1960; Nello Bemporad, architect, acting director December 1960–March 1961; Ferdinando Rossi, engineer and architect, 1961 to the present.

Master craftsmen: Conti, Orazio; Mannucci, Guido; Freni, Antonio; Massai, Enrico; Bettaccini, Lorenzo; Bichi, Italo; Gabbrielli, Giovanni; Vaggelli, Raffaello; Toti, Vittorio; Biliotti, Azelio; Bini, Marcello; Ciampi, Renzo; Bresci, Renato;

Mecocci, Alessandro; Viciani, Giuliano; Mangani, Affortunato; Ballini, Paolo; Toti, Alessandro; Ciuffi, Alessandro; Montanucci, Romolo; Ragazzini, Romano (economic secretary); Taddei, Gino; Biondi, Renzo; Fabbri, Aligi; Sarti, Cesare; Venturini, Giovanni; Mazzoni, Paolo; Cozzi, Paolo; Drovandi, Orano; Benucci, Danilo; Peschi, Oliviero; Agnoletti, Carlo; Agostini, Franco; Frizzi, Piero; Biliotti, Carlo; Innocenti, Piero; Gori, Romano; Barlondi, Galliano; Portolani, Libio; Martorana, Francesco (economic secretary); Raddi delle Ruote, Giancarlo; Bigazzi, Mario.

Inspectors: Annapaula Pampaloni Martelli, architect and vice-director.

Technical Chiefs: Angelo Del Sarto, Alfonso Biliotti.

Technical Assistant: Attucci, Giotto.

56 Principal marriages and connections of the Medici Grand Dukes of Tuscany (from G. F. Young, *op. cit.*, vol. II, table II):

- 1539 Cosimo I (1519–1574)
  Eleonora of Toledo

- 1565 Francesco I (1541–1587)
  Joanna, Archduchess of Austria

- 1574 Pietro, son of Cosimo I (1554–1604)
  Eleonora, daughter of Don Garcia of Toledo

- 1579 Francesco I (2nd marriage)
  Bianca Cappello of Venice

- 1583 Eleonora, daughter of Francesco I
  Vincenzo Gonzaga, Duke of Mantua.

- 1589 Ferdinando I (1549–1609)
  Christine of Lorraine

- 1600 Maria, daughter of Francesco I (1575–1642)
  Henry IV, King of France

- 1608 Cosimo II, son of Ferdinando I (1590–1620)
  Maria Maddalena, sister of the Emperor Ferdinando II

- 1620 Claudia, daughter of Ferdinando I (1604–1648)
  1 Federico della Rovere of Urbino
  2 Archduke Leopold of Austria

- 1628 Margherita, daughter of Cosimo II (1612–1662)
  Edoardo Farnese, Duke of Parma.

- 1634 Ferdinando II, son of Cosimo II (1610–1670)
  Vittoria della Rovere

- 1642 Anna, daughter of Cosimo II (1616–1660)
  Ferdinand Charles of Austria (her cousin)

- 1661 Cosimo III, son of Ferdinando II (1642–1723)
  Margherita Louisa of Orleans

- 1688 Ferdinando III, son of Cosimo III (1663–1713)
  Violante Beatrice of Bavaria

- 1697 Gian Gastone, son of Cosimo III (1671–1737)
  Anna Maria of Saxe-Lauenburg

- 1691 Anna Maria (Luisa) Ludovica, daughter of Cosimo III (1667–1743)
  William, Palatine Elector.

57 The School of Prague was established during the reign of the Holy Roman Emperor Rudolph II, *b.* Vienna 1552, *d.* Prague 1612. He was crowned King of Bohemia in 1575 and Emperor in 1576. He was a patron of both arts and sciences, and was himself knowledgeable in chemistry, alchemy, astronomy and astrology. In Bohemia, good quality jasper was discovered and much used.

BIBLIOGRAPHY

Aloisi, P., 'In Liburni Civitas', *Liburni Civitas a. VII*, fasc. I, p. 71 ff., 1934.

Agazzi, A., *Il mosaico in Italia*, Milan, 1926.

Aurigemma, S., 'L'Italia in Africa', Part I, *I Mosaici*, Rome, 1960.

Baldinucci, F., *Delle notizie de' professori del disegno*, Vol. XI, Florence, 1771.

Bartoli, L., *Dieci anni di attività dell' Opificio delle Pietre Dure dal 1950 al 1959*, Prato, 1960.

Bartoli, L. and Maser, E. A., *Il museo dell' Opificio delle Pietre Dure di Firenze*, Prato, 1954.

Becatti, G., *Scavi d'Ostia*, Rome, 1961.

Berchem, M. van and Clouzot, E., *Mosaiques Chrétiennes*, Geneva, 1924.

Berti, L., *Il Principe dello Studiolo*, Florence, 1967.

Berti, L., 'Matteo Nigetti', *Rivista d'Arte*, Florence, 1950.

Bettini, S., *La pittura Bizantina, i mosaici*, Florence, 1939.

Board of Heraclea: Bitola, *Mosaico pavimentale del Narthex di Eraclea*, Belgrade, 1967.

Bottari, S., *I mosaici della Sicilia*, Catania, 1942.

Bovini, G., *Mosaici di Ravenna*, Milan, 1956.

Brauns, R., *Il regno minerale*, Milan, 1905.

Brown, Blanche R., *Ptolemaic paintings and mosaics and the Alexandrian style*, Cambridge, Massachusetts, 1957.

Bussagli, M., *Forma e colore n. 52*, Florence, 1967.

Canarache, V., *Muzeol de archeologie din Constanta*, Bucharest, 1967.

Carobbi, G., *Lezioni di mineralogia*, Florence, 1951.

Cavenago, S. and Moneta, B., *Gemmologia*, Milan, 1959.

Cinotti, M., *Arte di tutti i tempi*, Novara, 1955.

Corsi Romano, F., *Dalle pietre antiche*, Rome, 1845.

Ducati, P., *L'arte classica*, Turin, 1939.

Enciclopedia Italiana, Rome, 1934.

Enciclopedia Universale dell' arte, Florence, 1963.

Fasiolo, O., *I mosaici di Aquileia*, Rome, 1915.

Fasolo, F. and Gullini, G., *Il Santuario della Fortuna Primigenia a Palestrina*, Rome, 1953.

Fiocco, G., *Torcello*, Venice, 1940.

Galassi, G., *Roma o Bisanzio*, Rome, 1953.

Gerspach, V., *La mosaïque*, Paris, 1878.

Gianfreda, Mons. G., 'Il mosaico pavimentale della Basilica Cattedrale di Otranto', *Abbazia di Casemari (Frosinone)*, 1965.

Giovannozzi, V., 'La vita di Bernardo Buontalenti scritta da Gherardo Silvani', *Rivista d'arte*, Florence, 1932.

Golzio, V., *Il seicento ed il settecento*, Turin, 1950.

Gullini, G., *I Mosaici di Palestrina*, Rome, 1956.

Landi, A., *I e R. Galleria dei lavori di commesso in pietre dure*, Florence, 1858.

Lavagnino, E., *L'arte medioevale*, Turin, 1953.

Levi, D., *Mosaici pavimentali di Antiochia*, London, 1945.

Maggiora, C., 'Il museo delle Pietre Dure in Firenze', *Bollettino tecnico degli Architetti e Ingegneri della Toscana*, Florence, Oct-Nov 1956.

Marchionni, E., *Osservazioni sul nuovo ordinamento della R. Manifattura del commesso in pietre dure*, Florence, 1861.

Matthiae, G., *Mosaici medioevali nelle chiese di Roma*, Rome, 1967.

Milani, G. B. and Fasolo, V., *Le forme architettoniche*, Milan, 1931.

Morassi, A., *Il tesoro dei Medici*, Milan, 1963.

Paatz, W. and E., *Die kirchen von Florenz*, Frankfurt, 1952–1955.

Petrasch, E., *Schloss Favorite Karlsruhe*, 1960.

Peyrot, A. and Maddalena, M., *Minerali e rocce*, Turin, 1963.

PIACENTI ASCHENGREEN, CHRISTINA, *Il museo degli Argenti*, Florence, 1967.
RODOLICO, F., 'Terminologia vasariana, nomi di pietre', extract from: *Lingua Nostra*, Florence, 1963.
ROSSI, FERDINANDO, 'Gioielli e pietre dure alla corte medicea', *Antichità e Belle Arti*, Florence, 1966.
ROSSI, FERDINANDO, 'L'Opificio delle Pietre Dure', *Antichità e Belle Arti*, Florence, 1962.
ROSSI, FERDINANDO, 'Trasformazione di antiche chiese conventuali fiorentine nel tardo Rinascimento', *Bollettino Ingegneri*, n. 12, Florence, 1965.
ROSSI, FERDINANDO, 'L'atelier des pierres dures des Médicis', *Connaissances des arts*, n. 167, Paris, Jan. 1966.
ROSSI, FILIPPO, *Capolavori dell'oreficeria italiana*, Milan, 1956.
SALVINI, *Mosaici medioevali in Sicilia*, Florence, 1949.
SANPAOLESI, P., 'Notizie documentatie sul Buontalenti', *Palladio*, Rome, Jan–March 1951.
SOULIER, G., *Les influences orientales dans la peinture toscane*, Paris, 1924.
TESCIONE, G., *Il corallo nella storia e nell' arte*, Naples, 1965.
TESCIONE, G., 'Il laboratorio delle pietre dure di Napoli e l'altare della Cappella Palatina della Reggia di Caserta', Extract from: *Studi in onore di Riccardo Filangieri*, vol. III.
TOESCA, P., *Storia dell' Arte Italiana*, Turin, 1914 and 1927.
TOESCA, P. and FORLATI, F., *Mosaici di San Marco*, Milan, 1957.
TRENTA, G., *I mosaici del Duomo di Pisa ed i loro autori*, Florence, 1896.
VENTURI, A., *Mosaici cristiani di Roma*, Florence, 1958.
WILPERT, J., *Die Römischen mosaiken und malereien Freiburg im Breisgau*, 1916.
WITT, A. DE, *I mosaici del Battistero di Firenze*, Florence, 1954.
YOUNG, G. F., *I Medici*, Florence, 1949.
ZOBI, A., *Notizie storiche sull' origine dei lavori di commesso in pietre dure che si eseguiscono nell' I. e R. Galleria dei lavori di commesso in pietre dure*, Florence, 1853.

SOURCES OF ILLUSTRATIONS

Bertoni, Florence; La Scala, Florence; Idea, Florence; Brogi, Florence; Federico Borromeo, Florence; Giorgio Nimatallah, Milan; Staatliche Museum, Berlin; Kunsthistorisches Museum, Vienna; Meier, Vienna; Courtesy of the Trustees of the British Museum, London; Istituto Centrale del Restauro, Rome; Gabinetto fotografico Nazionale, Rome; Plates 68, 72, 76, 77, 82, 86, 91–95, 97–99, 101, 102 are reproduced by kind permission of the Banca Toscana.

INDEX

INDEX OF NAMES

Numbers in italic refer to the captions to the illustrations

Abbas the Great, Shah, 17
Agatho, Pope, 66
Agnello, Bishop, 43
Ahmed Shah Durani, 150
Akbar, 17
Albatini, Guido Ubaldo, 82
Alberti, Leon Battista, 97
Alessandro, Duke, 124
Alexander the Great, 23, 25
Almeyda, Father Xavier de, 142
Ammirato, Benedetto, 118
Andrea, Zaccaria d', 55
Antoninus, 33
Appollonius, 53
Archias of Corinth, 16
Archimedes, 16
Aristeides of Thebes, 23
Arjumand Banu Begum, 146
Arnolfo di Cambio, 97
Arpino, Cavalier d', 82, 84
August George, Margrave of Baden-Baden, 160
Augustus, 30, 32
Austin of Bordeaux, 151
Autelli, Jacopo, 130, 139, 190
Azevedo, Michelangelo Cagianodi, 93, 188
Azurrio, Giovanni, 26

Baldinucci, F., 117, 133, 135, 137, 139, 188, 189
Baldovinetti, Alessio, 55, 80
Barbatelli, Bernardino, 130, 137, 190, *see also* Poccetti
Barberini, Cardinal Francesco, 26
Bartoli, Lando, 189, 192
Beauveau, Prince of Craon, Count of Richecourt, 162
Becatti, Giovanni, 30, 31, 32, 33, 184, 187
Beccafumi, Domenico, 98, 54
Belloni, 86
Benedict XIII, Pope, 82
Berzelius, Jacob, 105
Bianchi, Giovanni, 126, 190
Bianchi, Giovanni Junior, 139
Bianco, Baccio del, 139

Bilivert, Giacomo, 189
Bilivert, Giovanni, 189, 190
Bilivert, Jacopo, 126, 130, 137, 139, *69, 70*
Bona of Savoy, 124
Bordenache, Richard, 187
Borromini, Francesco, 100
Bottini, Giovanni Francesco, 139, 190
Bottini, Lorenzo, 139, 190
Bovini, G., 187
Brunelleschi, 118
Buglioni, Santi, 100, *59*
Buontalenti, Bernardo, 124, 126, 128, 133, 188, 189, 190
Bussagli, Mario, 16, 146, 150, 187, 189

Calandra, 26
Camerino, Jacopo da, 69
Campi, Francesco, 139, 191
Cappello, Bianca, of Venice, 193
Cardi, Ludovico, 128, 189, 190, *see also* Cigoli
Carlo, Carlieri, 173
Carlo, Giorgi, 173
Castrucci, Cosimo, 179
Castrucci, Giovanni, 179
Cavallini, Pietro, 69, 73, 74, 188, *39*
Celano, 141, 189
Celli, Benedetto, 139
Centelli, Carlo, 139
Cesari, Giuseppe, 82, *see also* Arpino
Charles III, King of France, 141
Charles VI, Emperor, 152
Charles Frederick, Margrave of Baden-Baden, 160
Chastel, André, 100, 188
Chermer, Cosimo, 139
Chiari, Pietro, 139
'Chimico, il', 139
Christine of Lorraine, 193
'Cigoli, il', 128, 133, 135, 137, 139, 189, 190, *69, 70*, *see also* Cardi
Cimabue, 53, 56, 80
Cinotti, Mia, 187
Cioci, Antonio, 164, 167, 191
Cioci, Leopoldo, 164, 167, 168, 191
Claudius, Emperor, 33

Clement VII, Pope 121, 124
Clement VIII, Pope, 82
Clouzot, E., 187
Compagni, Domenico, 121
Constantine the Great, 38, 76
Constantine V, Emperor of Byzantium, 76
Corniole, Giovanni delle, 121
Corso, Filippo di, 55
Cozzi, Pietro, 139
Cosimo I, *see* Medici
Cosimo II, *see* Medici
Cosimo III, *see* Medici
Curtius, Quintus, 22

Dandolo, Andrea, 50
Dandolo, Doge Enrico, 50, 53
Darius, 23
Delfe, Jacopo, 126
Della Rovere, Federico, Duke of Urbino, 193
Della Rovere, Vittoria, 193
Diodorus Siculus, 22
Dioscorides of Samos, 12
Donatello, 118
Donato, Donato di, 55
Dosio, Giovan Battista, 100
Ducati, Pericle, 22, 23, 42, 187
Dupré, Giovanni, 173

Eleonora of Toledo, 193

Fabiano Tommaso di 189
Fanciullacci Marco 142
Fanzago Cosimo, 100
Farnese, Edoardo, Duke of Parma, 193
Fasolo, Furio, 13, 187
Ferdinando I, *see* Medici
Ferdinando II, *see* Medici
Ferdinando III, *see* Medici
Ferdinand Charles, Emperor of Austria, 193
Feroni, Paolo, 177, 192
Ferrucci, Francesco, 137, 190
Foggini, Giovan Battista, 160
Forlati, F., 47, 50, 187
Francesco I, *see* Medici

196

Francesco II, *see* Medici
Francesco I, King of the two Sicilies, 173, 193
Francis, Grand Duke of Lorraine, 162, 167, 177, 189

Gaddi, Galdo, 53
Gaetani, Cardinal, 65
Gaffurri, Bernardino, 142
Garibaldi, 177
Garuffi, Giorgio, 126
George of Antioch, Patriarch, 75
Gérard, Baron, 86
Gerspach, V., 23, 69, 82, 86, 187, 188
Ghiberti, 118
Ghinghi, Francesco, 141
Giachetti, Giovanni, 139, 190 s
Giambologna (Jean Boulogne), 130
Gian Gastone, *see* Medici
Gianfreda, Mons. Grazio, 188
Giorgi, Giovan Battista, 167, 168, 171, 173, 177, 191, *92, 93*
Giorgi, Giovanni, 139, 190
Giotto, 56, 69, 73, 80, 97, 99, *40, 52*
Giovanni da Castel Bolognese, 121
Goetz, Herman, 17, 102, 187, 188
Golzio, Vincenzo, 188
Gregory IX, Pope, 65
Gregory XIII, Pope, 82
Gullini, Giorgio, 12, 23, 26, 27, 28, 31, 187

Hadrian, Emperor, 33, 34
Helena, daughter of Timon, 23
Henry IV, King of France, 193
Hieron II, 16
Honorius I, Pope, 66
Honorius III, Pope, 66

Iacopucci, Giovan Battista, 162
Ippolito, Priest, 66

Jahan, Shah, 102, 146, 151
Jahangir, 17
Joanna, Archduchess of Austria, 193
Jodi, Sikandar, 17
John VII, Pope, 66
John XXII, Pope, 66, 69
Julius Caesar, 94
Julius Francis, Duke of Saxe-Lauenberg, 154
Justinian, Emperor of Byzantium, 45, 80

Keyssler, J. C., 159
Kitzinger, E., 76, 80, 86, 187, 188

Lavagnino, E., 37, 45, 47, 65, 69, 75, 76, 187, 188
Leo X, Pope, 121
Leonardo da Vinci, 124
Leopold of Tuscany, Prince, Cardinal, 139
Leopold, Archduke of Austria, 193
Leopold, Grand Duke of Lorraine, 167

Leopoldo, I, Emperor, 154, 191
Leopoldo, Grand Duke of Tuscany, 177
Liberius, Pope, 66
Ligozzi, Jacopo, 126, 128, 137, 139, 190, *73*
Lorenzo the Magnificent, 121, 124
Lorenzo, Deacon, 66
Louis XV, King of France, 162
Louis-Philippe, King of France, 173
Louis-William, Margrave of Baden-Baden, 152, *see also* 'Türkenlouis'
Ludwig George, Prince, 159, 160

Maccari, L., 55
Maestro della Maddalena, 55
Mamurra, 94
Manenti, Vincenzo, 73
Marchionni, Eduardo, 55, 192
Marcutt, Marcutt di, 189
Margherita Louisa of Orleans, 193
Maria Teresa, 162
Marchionni, Edoardo, 177
Martini, Francesco di Giorgio, 99
Mascaccio, 80
Matteo di Giovanni, 98
Matthiae, Guglielmo, 65, 66, 69, 73, 188
Mazarin, Cardinal, 84
Medici, 118, 121, 124, 126, 128, 159, 160, 162, 179, 184, 189, *67*; Anna, 193; Anna Maria Ludovica, 162; Claudia, 193; Cosimo I, 121, 124, 128, 137, 190, 193; Cosimo II, 130, 151, 190, 193; Cosimo III, 139, 142, 152, 190, 191, 193; Eleonora, 193; Ferdinando I, 128, 130, 133, 142, 177, 190, 193; Ferdinando II, 133, 137, 139, 142, 151, 160, 167, 190, 193; Ferdinando III, 168, 177, 191, 193; Francesco I, 124, 126, 128, 142, 190, 193; Francesco II, 191; Gian Gastone, 139, 159, 162, 191, 193; Giovanni, 133, *see also* Ferdinando II; Giuliano, 121; Giulio, 124; Margherita, 193; Maria, 193; Maria Maddalena, 193; Pietro, 124, 193
Mellini, Cosma di Pietro, 88
Mellini, Deodato, 88
Mellini, Giovanni, 88
Mellini, Jacopo, 88
Mellini, Pietro, 88
Merlini, Andrea, 139
Merlini, Giovanni, 139
Metternich, Prince, 167
Michelangelo Buonarroti, 82, 84, 124, 188
Michelino, 121
Migliorini, Ferdinando, 139, 190, 191
Milani, G. B., 187
Minchioni, Giuseppe, 139, 191
Mochi, Francesco d'Orazio, 130, 190
Mochi, Orazio, 130, 190
Mohs, Friedrich, 105, 106, 108, 183, 185
Monnicca, 139

Montaigne, 126
Morassi, A., 121, 188
Muffati, Raffaello, 139, 190
Mussini, L., *56*
Muziano Gerolamo of Brescia, 82, 84

Nassaro, Matteo del, 121
Nemours, Giuliano, 124
Nicholas IV, Pope, 69
Nigetti, Matteo, 128, 133, 177, 189, 190

Orlandini, Amedeo, 55, 192
Otto II, Emperor, 66

Paatz, 53
Paolo da Venezia, 53
Partini, Ferdinando, 167, *89*
Passignano, Domenico, 137
Paurr, Cristoforo, 189
Pelagius II, Pope, 66
Peretti, Cardinal Andrea, 26
Pericoli, Nicolò, *see* Tribolo
Peruzzi, Benedetto, 118, 121
Petrasch, E., 160, 189
Pfleger, Franz, 159
Pietro (Berrettini) da Cortona, 82, 84
Pietro delle Opere, Lorenzo, 121
Pietro Leopoldo, Grand Duke, 164
Philoxenus of Eretria, 23
Pisano, Nicola, 80, 98
Pisano, Antonio, 121
Pius I, Pope, 65
Pius IX, Pope, 86
Pliny, 12, 16, 23, 25, 28, 31, 32, 93, 94, 187, 188
'Poccetti, il', 130, 137, 139, 190, *73*
Poggesi, 86
Poggini, Michele, 121
Pollaiulo, 121
Polo, Domenico di, 121
Pozzo, Cassiano del, 26
Provenzale da Cento, Marcello, 73, 82
Ptolemy of Hephaestion, 23
Ptolemy III, of Alexandria, 16
Ptolemy IV Philopater, 16
Pudenzio, Senator, 65
Pudenzio, Novatus, 65
Pudenzio, Timothy, 65

Quercia, Iacopo della, 121

Ramponi, Giuseppe, 142
Razzanti, Neri, 121
Riccio, Father Agostino del, 126
Rizzo, G. E., 22, 23, 25, 187
Roffia, Donato, 130
Rohrer, Michael Ludwig, 155
Rohrer, Peter Ernest, 154
Romanelli, Giovan Francesco, 84
Rossetti, Paolo, 84
Rossi, Domenico Egidio, 154, 159
Rudolph II, Emperor, 193
Ruggero II, King, 75, *44*
Rusuti, Filippo, 74

St Agnes, 66
St Anne, 69
St Apollinare, 46
St Augustine, *42*
St Francis Xavier, 142
St Gervasius, 45
St Gregory, *42*
St Lawrence, *42*
St Mark, *25*
St Martin, 43
St Matthew, 73
St Paul, 65, 66, 69
St Peter, 65, 66, 69, *42*
St Prazides, 65
St Protasius, 45
St Pudenziana, 65
St Silvester, *42*
St Vincent, *42*
San Miniato, 60
Sanguinetti, Michele, 159
Savonarola, 121, 124
Saxe-Lauenburg, Anna Maria Francesca of, 154, 159, 193
Serbaldi da Pescia, Pier Maria, 121
Sergius I, Pope, 66
Seriacopi, Cavaliere Giovanni, 126
Settimanni, Francesco, 130, 189
Sforza, Galeazzo, Duke of Milan, 124
Sibylla Augusta, Margravine of Baden-Baden, 152, 154, 159, 160
Siries, Carlo, 167, 168, 173, 177, 191
Siries, Cosimo, 162, 167, 191
Siries, Louis, 162, 164, 167, 191
Siries, Louis Junior, 167, 191
Sixtus III, Pope, 66
Sophilos, 16
Sosos of Pergamon, 12, 13, 17, 25

Soulier, Gustave, 97, 188
Stefano, Deacon, 66
Sulla, 12, 32

Tabaldo, Cosma, 88
Tabaldo, Jacopo, 88
Tabaldo, Lorenzo, 88
Tabaldo, Luca, 88
Tacca, Pietro, 130
Tafi, Andrea, 53
Taglicacarne, Giacomo, 121
Taylor, Bernard, 152
Tescione, Giovanni, 142, 189
Theodora, 45
Theodoric, 43, 47
Theodorus, Pope, 66
Theodorus, Bishop, *42*
Theodosius, Emperor of Byzantium, 37
Timon, 23
Toesca, Pietro, 37, 47, 50, 53, 187
Torricelli, Antonio, 160, 190
Torricelli, Gaetano, 160, 191
Torricelli, Giuseppe, 160, 190
Torrita, Jacopo (Fra Mino, Fra Jacopo), 53, 55
Torriti, Jacopo, 69
Trenta, G., 188
Tribolo, il, 100, 188, *59*
'Türkenlouis', 154, *see also* Louis-William

Umberto I, King of Italy, 192
Urban VIII, Pope, 82

Valle, Pietro della, 17
Varro, 32
Vasari, Giorgio, 53, 100, 121, 188
Vassalletti, Giovanni, 88

Vassalletti, Guittone, 88
Vassalletti, Niccolo, 88
Vassalletti, Ranuccio, 88
Venturi, Adolpho, 38, 187
Venturi, Luigi, 171
Veroneo, Geronimo, 148
Verrocchio, 121
Vicentino, Valerio, 121
Victor Emmanuel II, King of Italy, 177, 192
Victor Emmanuel III, King of Italy, 122
Vignola, Giacomo Barrozzi da, 102, 188
Vincenzo II, Pope, 66
Vincenzo Gonzaga, Duke of Mantua, 193
Violante Beatrice of Bavaria, 193
Violi, Filippo, 139, 191
Visconti, 31
Vitruvius, 32
Volterrano, 121

Wagner, Joseph, 164, 189
Werner, Abraham, 105
William, Elector Palatine, 162, 193
Witt, A. de, 55, 56, 60, 187, 188

Young, G. F., 142, 151, 152, 162, 188, 189, 193

Zobi, A., 117, 118, 126, 128, 130, 137, 139, 141, 142, 146, 150, 160, 171, 188, 189, 190, 191
Zocchi, Giuseppe, 162, 164, 167, 168, 177, 189, 191, *87, 88*
Zucconi, Giovanni Battista, 139, 190

INDEX OF PLACES

Abruzzi, the, 88
Aegean, 184
Afghanistan, 108
Africa, 108
Agra, 17, 146, 151, 152; Taj-Mahal, 102, 146, 148, 150, 151, *77*
Alexandria, 12, 16, 50; Museum, 16
America, 167
Andes, 108
Antioch, 75; Villa of Constantine, 37
Aosta, 80
Aquila, 100; Santa Maria di Collemaggio, 99
Aquileia, 11, 37, 38, 42, 43, *14*
Arbela, 23
Arizona, 108
Arles, 42
Asia, 102
Asia Minor, 16, 75, 93, 107, 182, 183
Athens, 94; Theatre of Dionysus, 94
Augsburg, 126
Austria, 37, 118, 142, 164
Azerbaijan, 17

Baalbek, 37
Baden-Baden, 152, 154
Baden Durlach, 160
Bagdhad, 17
Barcelona, 37, 124; Villa of Tossa del Mar, 37
Barga, 130
Bithynia, 107
Black Sea, 34, 107, *12, 13*
Bohemia, 154, 193
Bologna, 189
Bombay, 189
Boville Ernica, San Pietro Ispano, 73, *40*
Brindisi, 80
Byzantium, 16, 53, 60, 75, 76, 79, 90; see also Constantinople, Istanbul

Campania, 97, 184
Canada, 183
Capua, 88, 100; Cathedral, 88, *47*
Carthage, 34
Casale Monferrato, 80
Caserta, 141
Catabarbara, Sant' Agata dei Goti, 65; Sant' Andrea, 65
Cava dei Tirreni, 100
Calvi, 100
Caserta Vecchia, 100
Cava dei Tirreni, 88
Cefalu, 50, 75; Cathedral, *42*
Certaldo, 130
Chalcedon, 107, 182
Cherchel, 34
Chile, 108
China, 17, 108
Cologne, St Gereon, 80
Constanta, 34, *12, 13*
Constantinople, 50, see also Byzantium, Istanbul
Corsica, 108

Cremona, San Benedetto Po, 80
Crete, 93

Damascus, 16
Danube, 86
Daphni, 50
Delft, 126
Delhi, 17, 102, 151, 152

Egypt, 16, 17, 28, 93, 108
Empoli, Cathedral, 97
Ephesus, 37
Europe, 37, 80, 102, 108, 124, 142, 150

Fiesole, 160; Abbey, 97
Figeac, 162
Firenzuola, 130
Flanders, 133
Florence, 53, 55, 60, 86, 94, 97, 99, 100, 102, 117, 118, 121, 124, 126, 128, 130, 139, 142, 150, 160, 162, 177, 179, 184, 189, 192, *82*; Accademia della Crusca, 124; Campanile, 97, 99, *52*; Cathedral, 99, *53, 57, 58*; Fiorentina Gallery, 137; Laurentian Library, 100, *59*; Medici Chapel, 128, 130, 133, 173, 177, 189, *68*; Museo degli Argenti, 133, 189, *74, 76*; Museo dell' Opificio delle pietre dure, 133, 135, 160, 162, 164, 189, *60–63, 66, 67, 69–73, 78, 84, 85, 87–90, 94, 95*; Opificio delle Pietre Dure, 128, 130, 139, 142, 150, 151, 152, 160, 162, 164, 168, 173, 177, 189, 190, 192; List of all directors and workers from 1574–1970, 190–193; Palatine Chapel, 133; Palazzo Pitti, 121, 126, 162, 164, *74–76, 91, 92*; Palazzo Vecchio, 100; San Giovanni, Baptistry, 53, 59, 60, 80, 97, *26–28, 51*; San Lorenzo, Medici Mausoleum, 126, 130, 133, 135, 189, *93*; San Marco, Casino Mediceo, 124, 126, 128; San Miniato al Monte, 60, 80, 94, 97, *29*; San Niccolo, Convent, 168; Santa Maria del Fiore, see Cathedral; Santa Maria Novella, 97; Uffizi Gallery, 124, 133, 137, 192, *79*; Villa delle Cascine, 173; Villa del Poggio, 133
Folcide, San Luca, 50
Foligno, Abbey of Sassovivo, 88
France, 86, 108, 118, 139, 142, 152, 179

Gaul, 37, 94
Germania, 37
Germany, 108, 118, 126, 133, 154
Goa, 142, 189
Grado, 37
Greece, 26, 60, 75

Herculaneum, 20, 37, 94
Hippo, 34

India, 17, 102, 146, 151, 152, 189
Istanbul, 76, see also Byzantium, Constantinople; St Sophia, 76, *45*; St Irene, 76
Italy, 11, 16, 17, 25, 28, 29, 38, 74, 75, 80, 86, 102, 162, 182
Itimad Ud-Daulah, Tomb, 148

Jaipur, Fort of, 17
Jerusalem, The Dome of Rock, 16
Jumna, River, 146

Karlsruhe, 152, 160

Lahore, Fort of, 17
Lazio, 88, 97, 184
Leghorn, 142, 167; Fabbrica delle Pietre Dure, 142
Leningrad, 124
Liguria, 185
Lipari, 184
Lisbon, 142
Lombardy, 128
London, 124, 179; British Museum, 179, *5, 102*; Westminster Abbey, 88
Lucca, 63, 97; San Michele, 97
Lyons, 37

Madagascar, 108
Madrid, 37, 124; Prado, Museum, 179, 97; Villa of Aletejo, 37
Magna Graecia, 16
Malabar, 189
Marches, the, 88
Marmora, Sea of, 107
Mediterranean, 79
Mesopotamia, 37, *4*
Milan, 53, 126, 189
Monreale, 47, 50, 75, 76; Cathedral, *43*
Montecatini, 173
Murano, Santa Maria e Donato, 47
Mysia, 17

Naples, 23, 80, 100, 124, 139, 141, 184; Charter-house of San Martino, 100, 139; National Museum, 23, *7, 8*; Opificio, 139, 142; Parthenopean Institute, 141; Palatine Chapel, 142; Real Casa, 141; San Carlo alle Mortelle, 141; San Giovanni in Fonte, 80; San Prisco, 80; Santa Maria Capua Vetere, 80
New Mexico, 108
Nicaea, Church of the Dormition, 76
Nile, 16, 28, 86
Novara, 80

Orvieto, Cathedral, 86, 97; Tomb of Cardinal de Braye, 97
Ostia, 30, 31, 32, 33, 34, 45, 65, 66, 94, *11*; San Paolo, Basilica, 65, 69; Palazzo di Gamala, 31; Palazzo Imperiale, 31, 33
Otranto, Cathedral, 80, *46*; Oratory of Casa Ramello, 80

199

Padua, 118
Palermo, La Martorana, 75, 76, *41, 45*; 'Sacred Palace', 76; Santa Maria del' Ammiraglio, 75
Palestine, 37
Paphlagonia, 107
Parenzo, Cathedral, 46
Paris, 86, 124, 148; Louvre, 84, 86; Bibliothèque Nationale, 148; St Denis, 80
Pavia, 80, 128; Charter-house, 128; San Michele, 80
Pergamon, 17
Persia, 17, 108
Pesaro, 80
Phrygia, 107
Pisa, 53; Cathedral, 63, 97; San Nicola, 189
Piacenza, San Savino, 80
Piazza Armerina, 37
Po, River, 86
Pompeii, 12, 20, 21, 25, 37; House of the Coloured Capitals, 33; House of the Faun, 21, 23, 25, *6*
Praeneste, Palazzo Baronale, 26; Sanctuary of Fortuna Primigenia, 12, 26, 27, 28, *9, 10*
Prague, 179, 193, *99, 100*
Propontis, 107
Purana Kila, 17

Rastatt, 152, 154, 160; 'Favorite', Palace, 152, 154, 159, 160, *78–83, 86*
Ravello, Cathedral, 100
Ravenna, 38, 43, 45, 46, 47, 63, 76, 80; Archiepiscopal Chapel, 45; Baptistry of the Arians, 45; Baptistry of the Cathedral, 45; Cathedral of Ursis, 47; Galla Placidia, Mausoleum, 43, *15, 16*; Orthodox Baptistry, 94; San Giovanni Evangelista, 47, 80; San Peter in Classe, 47; San Vitale, 45, *17–20*; Sant' Agata, 47; Sant' Apollinare in Classe, 45, *23*; Sant' Apollinare Nuovo, 43, *21, 22*; Santa Croce, 47; Santa Maria Maggiore, 47
Reims, 37, 80; St Rémy, 80
Rhine, 152
Rome, 17, 20, 26, 28, 29, 31, 34, 38, 53, 63, 65, 66, 69, 74, 75, 76, 82, 84, 86, 88, 94, 100, 108, 184, 189; Capitoline Jupiter, Temple, 63, 94; Gregorian Chapel, 82; Junius Bassus, Basilica, 94; Lateran Baptistry, 65, 94; Lateran Museum, 12; Piazza del Esquilino, 63; Sant' Agnese, 63, 66, 94, *34*; Sant' Angelo, castel, 100; Sant' Antonio, 88; Santa Cecilia in Trastevere, 97; San Cesareo, 84; San Clemente, Basilica, 66, 82, 84, *35*; Santa Constanza, Basilica, 63, 65, 94, *30, 31*; Santi Cosma e Damiano, 66; San Damaso, 82; San Gerolamo della Carità, 100; San Giorgio al Velabro, 94; San Giovanni in Laterano, 69, 88; San Lorenzo Fuori le Mura, Monastery, 56, 88, *37*; San Luca, 84; Santa Maria in Cosmedin, 88; Santa Maria in Trastevere, 66, 69, *39*; Santa Maria Aracolei, 88; Santa Maria Maggiore, 63, 66, 69, 74, *38*; Santa Maria Nuova, 66; San Paolo Fuori le Mura, 50, 66, 88, 97; St Peter's, 65, 66, 74, 82, 84; San Prassede, *33, 36*; Santa Pudenziana, 53, 65, *32*; Santa Sabina, 65; SS. Sacramento, chapel, 82; San Sebastiano, Chapel, 82; Santo Stefano Rotondo, 66, 94; San Teodoro, 65, 66; San Tommaso in Formis, 88; San Venanzio, 66; Vatican, 66, 73, 80, 82, 84
Russia, 108

Saint-Romain, 37
Salerno, Cathedral, 88, 100
Salonika, 47, 76; Rotonda of St George, 47; St Sophia, 76
Santorini, 184
Saxe-Lauenburg, 154
Scarperia, 130
Schlackenwerth, Castle, 154
Ser Sah, Mosque, 17
Sessa Aurunca, Cathedral, 88, 100
Sicily, 16, 47, 59, 74, 75, 88
Siena, 68; Cathedral, 97, 99, *54–56*; San Domenico, 99
South Africa, 108
Spain, 118, 142, 179
Spalato, Palace of Diocletian, 37
Sumeria, 16
Syracuse, 16
Syria, 16, 37

Tabriz, 17
Tell Timai, 16
Terracina, 88, 100
Tivoli, Baths and Villa of Hadrian, 25, 37
Torcello, Chapel of the Blessed Sacrament, 47
Turin, 80
Tuscany, 53, 63, 82, 97, 124, 128, 130, 139, 141, 142, 152, 162, 177, 184

Umbria, 88
Ur, 13
Urals, 108
Uruk, 13, *4*; Eanna, Palace, 13
Utica, House of the Cascade, 34

Venice, 38, 47, 50, 53, 74, 75, 94, 164, 189; San Marco, Baptistry, 47, 50, 53, 74, 75, 94, *24, 25, 49*; Sant' Isidoro, chapel, 50
Vienna, 37, 124, 154, 162, 164, 167, 193; Kunsthistorisches Museum *99–101*
Volterra, 130

Warka, 13, *see also* Uruk

Zisa, 76